Venetian wealth depicted in the Pala d'Oro, St Mark's Basilica

cargoes of exotic goods to the dour lives of Lombards in the Po Valley and beyond the Alps to the courts of northern Europe.

Naples held on to its autonomy by combining links with Rome and Constantinople. When Arabs conquered Sicily in the 9th century and turned to the mainland, Naples sought an alliance. But as the invaders advanced towards Rome, Naples linked up with the then powerful maritime republic of neighbouring Amalfi. Despite military expeditions by the Franks and Byzantines, the Arabs remained on the Italian scene for two centuries, leaving a lasting influence on sciences and food.

The Middle Ages

In the 11th century, the adventurous Normans put an end to Arab control of Sicily and southern Italy. Exploiting a natural genius for assimilating the useful elements of the local culture rather than indiscriminately imposing their own, they adopted Arab-style tax collectors and customs officials and Byzantine admirals commanded their navy. In Palermo, churches and mosques stood side-by-side, feudal castles next to Oriental palaces and gardens.

The 13th-century fortifications at Colle di Val d'Elsa, Tuscany

The Crusades against Islam brought great prosperity to Italy's port cities. Pisa sided with the Normans in Sicily and profits from its new commercial empire in the western Mediterranean paid for its magnificent cathedral, baptistry, and campanile (the Leaning Tower). Genoa's equally powerful merchant empire spread from Algeria to Syria.

Supreme master of the art of playing all sides, Venice stayed out of the First Crusade to expand its trade with the faraway East while ferrying pilgrims to Palestine. In 1204, when Byzantium threatened its eastern trading privileges, Venice persuaded the armies of the Fourth Crusade to attack Constantinople; the conquest of Byzantium strengthened its position even further.

The Po Valley's economic expansion through land clearance and new irrigation works brought a rapid decline of feudalism. Dukes, administrators and clergy lived in towns rather than isolated castles, absorbing the hinterland into communes, forerunners of the city-states.

The Guelfs and the Ghibellines

The communes were strong enough to confine German Emperor Frederick Barbarossa's Italian ambitions to the south, where he secured Sicily for his Hohenstaufen heirs by marrying his son into the Norman royal family. Ruling from Palermo, Barbarossa's highly cultured but brutal grandson Frederick II (1194–1250) was a prototype for the future Renaissance prince.

His power struggle with the papacy divided the country into two highly volatile camps – Guelfs supporting the pope and Ghibellines supporting the emperor. The backbone of the Guelfs was in communes such as Florence and Genoa. In 1266, they financed the mercenary army of Charles d'Anjou to defeat the imperial forces – and take the Sicilian throne. But Palermo rose up against the French in the murderous Sicilian Vespers of 1282, when the locals massacred everyone who spoke Italian with a French accent and forced Charles to move his capital to Naples. The Sicilians offered their crown to the Spanish house of Aragon.

The Guelf-Ghibelline conflict became a pretext for settling family feuds (such as the one between the Montagues and Capulets in Shakespeare's *Romeo and Juliet*) or communal rivalries, from which Genoa and Florence emerged stronger than ever. In Rome, the dissolute popes repeatedly switched factions for temporary advantage and lost all political and moral authority.

Francis of Assisi

After two centuries of religious heresy, the Church needed spiritual renewal, finding the perfect ally in Francis of Assisi (1182–1226), pious without being troublesomely militant. His sermons had immense popular appeal. He chose not to attack Church corruption but instead to preach the values of a Christly life. The Franciscan order provided a much needed revival. The architecture of the church constructed in his name at Assisi contradicted Francis's humble testament denouncing 'temples of great dimension and rich ornament.' But Assisi's frescoes of the saint's life, painted by Cimabue and disciples of Giotto (which barely survived the severe earthquake of 1997), proved an immensely effective act of artistic propaganda against the prevalent libertinism and heresy.

St Francis Receiving the Stigmata by Tiepolo

The City-States

By the end of the 13th century, with the independent-minded communes growing into fully fledged city-states, Italy was not to be subjugated to the will of one ruler. The Middle Ages in Italy saw the founding of Europe's first university in Bologna in the 11th century, followed by institutions of learning in Padua, Naples, Modena, Siena, Salerno and Palermo. In the absence of political unification, it was the universities that awakened the national consciousness. Scholars who were travelling across the country needed a common tongue beyond the elitist Latin to break through the barriers of regional dialects. German Emperor Frederick II launched the movement for a national language at his court in Palermo, but Florentine-born Dante Alighieri (1265–1321) provided the ardour, moral leadership and literary example to bring it to fruition.

Dante Alighieri, literary giant

The maritime republic of Genoa rose to challenge Venice's supremacy. It dislodged Pisa in the western Mediterranean, whittled down Venice's hold on eastern ports, and set up colonies on the Black Sea for trade with Russia and faraway Cathay (China). But Genoa's participation in the ruinous Chioggia War of 1381 on the Venetian lagoon exhausted its resources.

Venice and its Repubblica Serena (Serene Republic) rebounded and turned to the mainland, extending its Veneto territory from Padua across the Po Valley as far as Bergamo. After relying exclusively on overseas trade, Venice created a new land-owning aristocracy through this expansion.

In the fertile Po Valley, Milan prospered from trade with Germany, principally in textiles and armour. Escaping unscathed from the Black Death of 1348 and subsequent plagues, it built up a sound economic base and maintained a strong army.

San Lorenzo Cathedral, Genoa

Florence was the first Italian town to mint its own gold coin (*fiorino* or florin), a prestigious instrument for trade in European markets, and it organised textile manufacture on a grand scale. Despite uprisings such as that of the *Ciompi* (wool-workers), the resilient Florentines were well-fed and highly literate compared to the residents of the rest of the country. The wealthy, ambitious Medici emerged as the dominant merchant family. Cosimo the Elder (1389–1464) became the city's ruler and founder of the Medici dynasty in 1434. A building boom underlined the prosperity: Giotto's Campanile was finally completed, as were Ghiberti's baptistry doors, and Brunelleschi's dome on the cathedral.

Divided in the 14th century between the Spanish in Sicily and the French in Naples, southern Italy remained solidly feudal. Its agricultural economy suffered more than the north from plague and drought, which brought the inevitable famine. As Palermo was in decline, Naples flourished as a brilliant cosmopolitan capital. It was reunited with Sicily and known as the Kingdom of the Two Sicilies under the Spanish King Alfonso V of Aragon in 1442.

With the papacy in comfortable exile in Avignon since 1309, the brutal rule of the Orsini and Colonna families reduced Rome to a half-urban, half-rural backwater village. Self-educated visionary Cola di Rienzo governed briefly in 1347 until the nobles drove him out. After 30 years, the papacy returned.

The High Renaissance

A new national fraternity of scholars with expertise in the arts, sciences and law emerged as itinerant consultants to visionary rulers eager to make their city-states centres of cultural prestige and political propaganda. Men such as Leon Battista Alberti, the brilliant architect-mathematician-poet, brought about a new spirit of inquiry and scepticism. From their detailed study and translation of the Greek philosophers, they developed principles of objective scientific research, independent of the political, religious and emotional bias of earlier times.

Leonardo da Vinci eagerly applied the new method to architecture, civil and military engineering, urban planning, geography and map-making. This cultural explosion was dubbed a *rinascita*, or rebirth, of the glories of Italy's Greco-Roman past. But even more, it proved, with the humanism of both Leonardo and Michelangelo and the political realism of Machiavelli, to be the birth of our modern age.

The spectacular ceiling of the Medici Chapel

Unfortunately, the creative ferment by no means precluded new horrors of war, assassination, persecution, plunder and rape. It was the heyday of the brilliant but lethal Spanish-Italian Borgias: lecherous Rodrigo, who became Pope Alexander VI, and treacherous son Cesare, who stopped at nothing to control and expand papal lands. His sister Lucrezia, forever smeared by anti-Spanish propaganda of the day as mistress of both her father and brother, was in fact,

Lorenzo 'il Magnifico' de' Medici, patron of the arts

as Duchess of Ferrara, a generous patron of the arts and benefactor of the poor.

In Florence, where his family had to fight to hold on to their supremacy, Lorenzo 'il Magnifico' de' Medici (1449–92) found time to encourage the art of Perugino, Ghirlandaio, Botticelli, young Leonardo and tempestuous Michelangelo.

On the international scene, the Turkish conquest of Constantinople in 1453 closed Genoa's Black Sea markets, but competitor Venice worked out a new deal in Cyprus and even a *modus vivendi* in Constantinople itself. But the Venetians' empire declined as they lost their taste for the adventure of commerce in favour of the safety of their landholdings. From 1494 to 1530, the Spanish Habsburgs and the French turned Italy into a battleground for the Kingdom of Naples and the Duchy of Milan. Genoa sided with the Spanish to give Emperor Charles V access, via Milan, to his German territories, and later became a lucrative clearinghouse for Spain's newly discovered American silver. Rome was plundered by imperial armies in 1527; the Medici were driven out of Florence and returned to power under tutelage of the Spanish, who won effective control of the whole country.

Michelangelo sculpture in the Medici Chapel, Florence

When the dust of war settled, it was the dazzling cultural achievements that left their mark on the age. The true father of Rome's High Renaissance, Pope Julius II (1503–13) began the new St Peter's cathedral, and commissioned Michelangelo to paint the ceiling of the Vatican's Sistine Chapel and Raphael to decorate the Stanze. Architect Donato Bramante was nicknamed *maestro ruinante* because of all the ancient monuments he dismantled to make way for the pope's megalomaniac building plans. With treasures uncovered in the process, Julius founded the Vatican's magnificent collection of ancient sculpture.

Counter-Reformation

Badly shaken by the Protestant Reformation in northern Europe, the Catholic Church convoked the Council of Trent (north of Lake Garda) in 1545. Non-Italian bishops urged the Church to carry out its own reform, hoping to democratise relations with the pope. But the threat of Lutherans, Calvinists, and other heretics shifted the emphasis to repression, culminating in the Counter-Reformation formally proclaimed in 1563. The Church reinforced the Holy Office's Inquisition and the Index to censor the arts. The Jesuits, founded in 1534, became an army of theologians to combat heresy. Italian Protestants fled and Jews in Rome were restricted to a ghetto (50 years later than the Venice ghetto, Europe's first) and expelled from Genoa and Lucca.

Cardinal Carlo Borromeo, nephew of Pope Pius IV and Archbishop of Milan (1565–1584), was the exemplary spiritual leader of Italy's Counter-Reformation. In alliance with the Jesuits, he weeded out corrupt clerics. As a symbol of his crusading spirit, he consecrated Milan's new Flamboyant Gothic cathedral, which took centuries to complete and remains one of the world's largest and most famous Gothic structures.

In the south, the 16th century saw Naples become the largest town in Europe – and one of the liveliest – but it was oppressed and impoverished. In Sicily and Naples the army crushed revolts against taxes and conscription for Spain's wars in northern Europe.

Towards Nationhood

Lacking the solidarity to unite and too weak to resist by themselves, Italian kingdoms and duchies were reduced to handy pawns in Europe's 18th-century dynastic power plays. At the end of the Wars of Spanish, Austrian, and Polish Succession, the Austrians had taken over northern Italy from the Spanish. The Age of Enlightenment engendered a new cultural ferment. In Milan, the theatre of La Scala opened, while La Fenice opened in Venice. Stimulated by the ideas of Voltaire, Rousseau, and Diderot, the country's intellectuals were more keenly aware of being not only Europeans, but also *Italians*.

The hopes of progressives were raised by Austrian reforms in Lombardy and Tuscany (where the Medici dynasty had finally fiz-

---

Cultural Propaganda

Art proved a major instrument of Counter-Reformation propaganda, but it had to undergo some important changes. The vigour and intellectual integrity of the High Renaissance had softened into the stylised sophistication of Mannerism, the transition from the Renaissance to the baroque. Condemning the preoccupation with pagan gods and decadence, the Church urged artists to deliver a strong, clear message to bring the troubled flock back to the fold. The Madonna and saints of Annibale Carracci further paved the way for the baroque, attracting the faithful with a sensuous image of ideal beauty, while Caravaggio made a more brutal, but no less effective, appeal with a proletarian Mary and barefoot Apostles.

The baroque Palazzo Reale in Turin, home to Savoy princes

zled out by 1737). The results included fairer taxes, less Church influence in schools, more public education and removal of the Inquisition, Jesuits, the death penalty and instruments of torture. Outside the Austrian sphere of influence, Italy remained solidly conservative. Venice stagnated under the rule of an entrenched élite, drawing nostalgic comfort from the city's beauty as painted in the *vedute* of Guardi and Canaletto. The papacy in Rome had lost prestige with the dissolution of the Jesuits and the crippling loss of revenue from the Habsburg Church reforms. The South's aristocracy resisted all significant social reforms proposed by the Spanish. Don Carlos, a descendant of Louis XIV, saw himself as a southern Sun King with Caserta Palace as his Versailles and is best remembered for launching the excavations of Pompeii in 1748.

On the northwestern Alpine frontier, a new state had appeared on the scene, destined to lead the movement to a united Italy. With Savoy split in the 16th century between France and Switzerland, its foothill region southeast of the Alps, Piedmont, had come into the Italian orbit. Sidestepping the stagnant economic burden of Spanish domination, the sparsely populated duchy expanded quickly. Turin was little more than a fortified village of 40,000 inhabitants in 1600, but it rose to 93,000 a century later. The pragmatic dukes of Piedmont favoured French-style absolutist monarchy tempered with a parliament to bypass local fiefdoms. They copied Louis XIV's centralised administration and tax-collection and, by the 18th century, Turin was a sparkling royal capital built, unlike any other Italian city, in classical French manner.

Napoleon's 'Liberation'

Napoleon Bonaparte, with his ideas of Italian 'independence', was welcomed after driving out the Austrians and Spanish in 1797. But the Italian treasuries were soon used to support the French war effort and the Bonaparte family. If Napoleon did not 'liberate' Italy, he did shake up the old conservatism from Lombardy to Naples by creating new universities and high schools, streamlining the bureaucracy, creating a new legal system with his Napoleonic Code, and awakening the forces of Italian nationalism.

Caution was the watchword among Italian rulers restored to their lands after Napoleon's defeat. Austria seized the chance to add the Veneto to its territories. The 1823 conclave elected arch-conservative Leo XII to help the papacy recover from its Napoleonic shock. On the lookout for any contagiously progressive movement, the Austrians helped Bourbon King Ferdinand of Naples crush an 1821 revolt for constitutional monarchy and foiled an uprising in Piedmont. In 1831 insurrection spread through Bologna, Modena and Parma to the Papal States of central Italy. But the Austrians defeated a rebel government of 'united Italian provinces', weakened by regional rivalries and conflicting personal ambitions.

Napoleon, champion of a new Italy

The Risorgimento

The Risorgimento, the 'resurrection' of national identity, took two conflicting paths. Genoese-born Giuseppe Mazzini's *Giovane Italia* (Young Italy) movement sought national unity by popular-based insurrection. He opposed Piedmontese patricians and intellectuals of the Moderates party, seeking reform through a privilege-conscious confederation of Italian princes blessed by the papacy – with Piedmont providing the military muscle. The Moderates feared a proletarian militancy among factory workers. Landowners bringing in cheap migrant day-labour faced peasant resentment. Food riots broke out in Lombardy, revolts in Tuscany, and southern peasants demanded a share of common land.

Outright rebellion erupted in Milan on 18 March 1848, the year of revolution across Europe. Emissaries flew by balloon to nearby cities for reinforcements that freed Milan from the 14,000-strong Austrian garrison. The Venetians restored their republic, a Piedmontese army joined with troops from Tuscany, the Papal States and Naples, and a new democratic Roman Republic was proclaimed. But the hesitant Carlo Alberto of Piedmont gave the Austrians time to re-establish their authority and Italian gains toppled. National unity was once again sabotaged by provincial rivalries.

Conceding the need for more reform, the new king of Piedmont, Vittorio Emanuele II, became a constitutional monarch with a parliament dominated by moderates. His Prime Minister, Count Camillo Cavour, was a hard-nosed political realist who won over left-wing support for a programme of free-trade capitalism and large-scale public works construction. Among the political exiles flocking to Piedmont was a veteran of the earlier revolts, Giuseppe Garibaldi.

The composer Giuseppe Verdi was the Risorgimento's towering artist. His operas' romantic humanism inspired fellow patriots, who saw in the Nabucco Freedom Chorus a positive call to action.

With their French allies, Piedmont defeated Austria at Magenta and Solferino to secure Lombardy in 1859. A year later, Cavour negotiated the handover of Emilia and Tuscany. But it was the adventure of Garibaldi's Red Shirts that imposed the unification of the peninsula in 1860. With two steamers, antiquated artillery, and 94,000 lire in funds, he set sail from Genoa with his 'Expedition of the Thousand'. The heroic Red Shirts seized Bourbon Sicily and crossed to the mainland. At Teano, outside Naples, they met Vittorio Emanuele, who was proclaimed the first King of Italy. National unity was completed with the annexation of the Veneto in 1866 and Rome was made the new capital in 1871.

Giuseppe Garibaldi

The Modern Era

Despite its extraordinarily fragmented history, unified Italy took its place among modern nations as an unexceptional centralised state. It was careful to protect the interests of its industrial and financial establishment and granted reforms to the working classes only under the pressure of their united action.

Both the politically left and the right wanted Italy to join the European race for colonies – their eyes fixed on Ethiopia and Libya. Conservatives supported expansion for reasons of national prestige. Socialists talked of Italy's 'civilising mission' in the Mediterranean, seeking to divert the flow of emigrants (heading increasingly to the Americas) to experimental collective land management in new African colonies in Tripoli and Cyrenaica.

At home, in addition to traditional textiles, industry was expanding fast in metallurgy, chemicals and machinery. The national love affair with cars had begun – from seven produced in

1900 and 70 in 1907, there were 9,200 rolling out of the factories by 1914, most of them from Fiat, which was founded in 1899.

With Prime Minister Giovanni Giolitti manoeuvering the capital and labour forces, Italy began its 20th century in a blithe state of calm and prosperity known as *Italietta*, and remained neutral when war broke out in 1914. The following year, acting with what Prime Minister Antonio Salandra acknowledged to be '*sacro egoismo*', Italy signed a secret treaty to enter the war on the side of Britain, France and Russia in exchange for the post-war annexation of Austrian-held Trento, South Tyrol (now Alto Adige) and Trieste.

The people were at first cool to the war, despite the jingoism of Fascist sympathiser, aristocrat and author Gabriele D'Annunzio and his friend, ex-socialist newspaperman Benito Mussolini. The Italian Army was the least well prepared of the combatants, lacking artillery, machine guns, trucks and trained officers, but the infantry showed great courage in the trenches. After the disaster at Caporetto, the planned Austro-German 1917 advance across the Veneto plain was held until the Italian counter-attack of October–November 1918 permitted a triumphant entry into Trento and Trieste. For most Italians, particularly the peasant, worker and petit bourgeois, war in uniform was their first real experience of Italian nationality. Keen war-supporters such as D'Annunzio, who captured the popular imagination by flying over Vienna to drop propaganda leaflets, were acclaimed as patriots, while democrats and pacifist republicans were dismissed as defeatists. Parliament, which was denied knowledge of the secret war treaty until the Peace Conference of 1919, was exposed as impotent.

The Rise of Fascism

The political left was in disarray. The Socialists won the elections but split over support for the Russian Revolution, leading to the formation in 1921 of the Italian Communist Party. In an atmosphere of economic crisis – stagnant productivity, bank closures and rising unemployment – conservatives wanted somebody tougher and more dynamic than the eternally compromising old-style politicians. As the black-shirted *Fasci Italiani di Combattimento* (Italian combat groups) beat up Slavs in Trieste and trade union workers in Bologna, Mussolini filled the role. Threatened by the Fascists' March on Rome in 1922, King Vittorio Emanuele III caved in and invited Mussolini, *il Duce*, to form a government.

The now all-too-familiar process of totalitarianism set in: opposition leaders were assassinated; their parties, free unions and the free press were abolished. Yet Italian Fascism remained more of a style than a coherent ideology, characterised by bombastic architecture and the arrogant harangues of Mussolini from the Palazzo Venezia's 'heroic balcony' in Rome.

Most Italians survived with lip-service and good humour, while Communists re-allied with Socialists in the anti-Fascist underground, whose partisans linked up with the Allies during World War II. In 1936, Mussolini diverted attention from the worsening economic climate at home with an invasion of Ethiopia and proclamation of the Italian Empire. Italian war planes joined Hitler's Luftwaffe on General Franco's side in the Spanish Civil War (5,000 Italian Communist and Socialist volunteers fought on the Republican side).

Following the Germans' lead in 1938, racist legislation was introduced against the country's 57,000 Jews. The next year, Italy invaded Albania and, after France's collapse in June 1940, plunged with Germany into World War II. Its poorly equipped armies were defeated by the British in the African desert and by the mountain snows in the Balkans. The Allies landed in Sicily in June 1943 and liberated Rome one year later. Mussolini, toppled soon after the Allied landings and re-instated briefly as a German puppet in the north, was

Mussolini the demagogue, 1935

Villa Feltrinelli in the Lakes where Mussolini ruled from 1943–5

caught fleeing in German uniform to the Swiss border. He was executed in April 1945.

The sordid hardships of post-war Italy – unemployment, the black market and prostitution – have been made graphically familiar through the cinema of Rossellini, de Sica and Fellini.

Post-War Recovery and the 21st Century

Today, the remarkable economic recovery has silenced the old condescension about Italy's technological and managerial talents. In the European Union (EU), Italy has more than held its own in heavy industry, agribusiness and the electronics industry. Italians didn't take easily to national government. They had existed through most of their history without it and Mussolini had spoiled their appetite. Fatigued by 'Il Duce's' excesses, they rejected the militant left for a little *dolce vita* with the less adventurous but less disturbing Christian Democrats. Their ever-changing coalitions hardly constituted real national government, but nevertheless, the population seemed to function quite well. In the 1980s, a pragmatic Socialist coalition government with the Christian Democrats brought a few years of unusual stability. Corruption and tax-evasion continued, but the police clamped down on the political terrorism of the Red Brigades and neo-Fascists and the age-old criminality of the Mafia.

As Italy put on its best face for the nationwide celebration of Jubilee 2000, a series of corruption scandals *(tangenti)* revealed the dirty and deep-rooted hold of politicians and business tycoons alike that began in the early to mid-1990s.

In a landslide victory in 2001, Silvio Berlusconi's centre-right government came to power on a tide of populism and nationalism, with a pledge to reform and liberalise the economy. But the country has since sunk into recession and floundered in protectionist measures.

In 2002, Italy, like most members of the EU, scrapped its own currency, the lira, and embraced the euro. Despite Berlusconi's assertion that it was in Italy's interest to adopt the euro, the country's experience has been unpromising, with the currency blamed for

Silvio Berlusconi, Italy's richest man

price rises, and seen as a cause of the country's economic problems rather than a symptom. Italy currently faces a spiralling budget deficit and towering national debt, the third highest in the world.

After a long illness John Paul II died in April 2005 and was succeeded by Pope Benedict XVI (formerly Cardinal Joseph Ratzinger), an arch conservative with unyielding views on birth control, sexuality and euthanasia.

Berlusconi was forced to resign in April 2005 after defeat in the regional elections, but gained a temporary reprieve by re-assembling his four-party Casa delle Liberta alliance. However, in the face of continued economic troubles, Berlusconi's centre-right coalition was defeated in the 2006 general elections.

Nevertheless, the opposition won by the smallest of margins. The centre-left coalition, led by Romano Prodi, the former EU President, may find it hard to push through its economic reforms given its weak parliamentary mandate. In addition, the coalition unites parties with very different agendas, including Catholics, former Communists and the Greens, so an ideological roller-coaster ride cannot be ruled out. Their plan is to liberalise the economy, inject greater flexibility in the job market and strengthen relations with the EU. But with such a small platform for reform, lifting the economy appears a difficult prospect.

Historical Landmarks

9th century BC First signs of pre-Roman Etruscans.

8th century BC Greeks colonise Sicily and other southern regions.

753BC Rome founded.

510BC Establishment of Roman Republic.

264–241BC Rome defeats Carthage in First Punic War.

44BC Julius Caesar assassinated on 15 March.

27BC Octavius (Caesar Augustus), the nephew and heir of Julius Caesar, founds the Roman Empire.

AD79 Vesuvius volcano buries Pompeii.

306–337 Emperor Constantine makes Constantinople the capital and Christianity the state religion.

410 Visigoths sack Rome.

476 The fall of the Roman Empire; the Dark Ages begin.

800 Pope crowns Charlemagne Holy Roman Emperor.

827–1060 Arabs invade and settle in Sicily.

1000–1100 Normans conquer south; First Crusade.

1282 Massacre of French settlers in the 'Sicilian Vespers'.

1309–1377 Papacy exiled from Rome to Avignon, France.

1378–1381 Maritime Republics Venice and Genoa fight for supremacy.

1442 Alfonso V of Aragon crowned king of 'Two Sicilies' (Naples and Sicily).

1494–1559 Spanish and French fight over Naples and Milan.

1503–1513 Rome is centre of the Renaissance.

1527 Sack of Rome by Imperial troops.

1545–1563 Council of Trent starts the Counter-Reformation.

1700–1713 War of the Spanish Succession ends and Austria becomes the major foreign power.

1796–1814 Napoleon invades north then much of Italy.

1815–1832 Austrians crush insurrection; the Risorgimento, a national political movement begins.

1831 Mazzini founds la Giovane Italia to combat Austria.

1848–1849 Abortive countrywide revolts.

1859 Franco-Piedmontese alliance takes Lombardy.

1860 Garibaldi's 'Thousand' conquer Naples and Sicily.

1861 Kingdom of Italy proclaimed with Turin as capital and Victor Emanuel II as king.

1871 Rome named capital of unified Italy.

1915 Italy joins British/French/Russians in World War I.

1919 Trento, South Tyrol (Alto Adige) and Trieste acquired from Austria.

1922 Mussolini begins Fascist regime with march on Rome, declaring himself Prime Minister, then Duce.

1929 Lateran Treaty establishes separate Vatican state.

1936 Mussolini annexes Abyssinia (Ethiopia).

1940 Italy joins Germany in World War II.

1943–1944 Allies liberate Sicily, then Rome; Mussolini arrested. Rescued by Germans, he founds puppet state in the North.

1945 Execution of Mussolini and his mistress.

1946 Abdication of Victor Emanuel III; proclamation of the Republic.

1957 Treaty of Rome institutes the EEC, forerunner of the European Union (EU), of which Italy is one of the six founder members.

1970s–80s Shadowy far-left group, the Red Brigade, causes instability in a campaign of kidnapping and murder.

1978 Former President, Aldo Moro, is murdered.

1981 Pope John Paul II is attacked in St Peter's Square.

1990 Swift rise of the secessionist Northern League.

Early 1990s Widespread economic and political corruption scandals. Two anti-Mafia judges assassinated in Sicily.

1992–1994 Umberto Bossi's Northern League and Silvio Berlusconi's centre-right Forza Italia party become significant political forces.

1997 Earthquakes hit Umbria causing serious damage.

2001 Media magnate Silvio Berlusconi is elected Prime Minister.

2002 The euro replaces the lira. An earthquake in Puglia kills 26 children.

2003 As part of 'New Europe', Italy backs the US on Iraq.

2005 Pope John Paul II dies. Cardinal Joseph Ratzinger is elected Pope Benedict XVI.

2006 Turin hosts the Winter Olympics. Romano Prodi and his centre-left coalition win the closely-fought general election. Police capture Italy's most-wanted man, Bernardo Provenzano, the suspected head of the Sicilian mafia.

WHERE TO GO

Planning a trip to Italy entails a series of difficult decisions. 'Doing' Italy is a lifetime's job and many devotees are so in love with the place that they won't even think of an alternative destination. After a predictable first romance with Rome, Venice or Florence, they spend the rest of their lives systematically working their way through the small but wildly varied country, region by region, visit after visit. If this is your first trip, you'll do well to establish an overall impression. If the seduction works – and it usually does – you'll want to come back time and again.

FIVE AREAS

This section includes all the most important towns and regions to help you make your choice. Each of the five areas has a principal city as a focus or starting point: **Rome** for central Italy, plus the island of Sardinia; **Florence** for Tuscany, with Umbria and the Adriatic seaside resorts to the east; **Venice** for Veneto, the Dolomites and Emilia Romagna's historic towns from Parma to Ravenna; **Milan** for Lombardy, Piedmont and the Italian Riviera to the west; and **Naples** for the south and Sicily.

Depending on how much time you have for that all-important first taste, we suggest you try to visit at least two, even three, of the regions. Those with a passion for the big city can combine Rome with the artistic delights of Florence and Tuscany, or Milan with the magical romance of Venice. For many, the key to Italy's Mediterranean soul is to be found in Naples and the south. When the summer heat gets too much (air conditioning is not always available), cool off at the seaside resorts of the Riviera, or any of the gem-like islands.

The trick is in the mix, not just geographically, in exploring the variety and contrasts of north and south, but in combining the attractions of town and countryside and the resultingly different facets of Italy's daily life. Nowhere is it easier or more delightful to overdose on museums and monuments than in Italy. A dear old lady returned from her first visit with the observation: 'Italy's very nice, very nice indeed, but for my taste, much too much history.'

While it would be a crime to ignore the churches, *palazzi* and museums chronicling the unparalleled glories of Italy's history, the best way to enjoy them is also to spend plenty of time soaking up the atmosphere from a front-row seat in a café, or from under a beach umbrella watching seaside life unfold. The siesta is one of the greatest of all Latin institutions and the most important Italian expression you may ever learn is *dolce far niente* (the sweetness of doing nothing).

Many people cannot manage to go to Italy outside the major holiday periods – Easter, July and August. But if your options are more flexible, the most enjoyable (slightly less crowded) months

Museum Tips

Museum-going in Italy is not always simple. Even the local tourist office cannot always keep up with the changes in opening hours. Some museums are closed temporarily – for days, months or even years – for *restauro* (restoration). This is a blanket term covering budgetary problems for museum staff and modern security systems, or genuine, long overdue programmes of renovation of the buildings and restoration of the paintings. Many ancient Roman monuments may also go into prolonged hiding under protective scaffolding.

When you visit one of the huge museums such the Uffizi or the Vatican, treat it like Italy itself: Unless you're a museum-fiend, don't try to see it all. Before you begin, study the museum plan at the entrance, then head for the things that capture your interest the most. Or, if you prefer the serendipity of coming across beautiful surprises, just wander around, but not for much more than a few hours. Otherwise, you may get a sharp attack of visual overload and won't be able to recall the next day, let alone years later, just what masterpieces you saw. Many cities offer cost-effective tourist passes that include entry to museums.

are May, June, September and
October – especially if you
are intending to visit Rome,
Venice and Tuscany. Certainly,
July and August can be almost
unbearably hot and humid in
most big cities, but some find
an odd, ghostly pleasure in
being in Rome on Ferragosto
(on and around 15 August)
when the city is abandoned 'to
the cats and the crazy.'

Stylish wheels, Polanza

Remember, that the Italians
make no bones about their
public holidays *(see page 238)* which are generally big family
affairs; they just shut up shop and close the whole country down.

GETTING AROUND

Even the most free-spirited traveller can use a little help occasionally. As tourism is such a vital factor in Italy's economy,
there is an elaborate network of information offices. Bureaucrats
being bureaucrats, efficiency and amiability vary from place to
place, but the tourist information offices all provide useful maps
and brochures.

For general information, the state tourist office ENIT *(Ente
Nazionale Italiano per il Turismo)* has offices in major foreign
cities as well as regional capitals. When in Italy, look instead for
the APT *(Azienda di Promozione Turistica)* for more detailed regional sightseeing information; they occasionally help as well
with hotel and camping accommodation. CIT *(Compagnia Italiana di Turismo)* is a national travel agency for transport, excursions and hotel bookings.

The Travel Tips section at the back of the book *(see page 222)*
gives detailed practical guidance on the technicalities of travel
through Italy, but here are some general thoughts to help you
plan your trip.

By Road and Rail

The most convenient, fastest and often cheapest way to travel is by train. The rail service is efficient and provides a stress-free route with the bonus of relaxed sightseeing en route. The local trains, 'Locale', meander, stopping at every station, while the faster Intercity, Eurocity and Eurostar are long-distance links between major cities, for which you pay a supplement. The Eurostar Italia (ES) has very fast rolling stock, including the tilting 'Pendolino'. The latest model, the non-tilting ETR 500, is currently capable of 185 mph (300 km/h). A network of high-speed lines that could reach 625 mph (1,000 km/h) by 2008 is also underway.

The great breathtaking Italian adventure is still the road. The *autostrada* (toll motorway) runs the length and breadth of the

Double decker train, Riomaggiore

peninsula, a challenge to the imagination and survival instincts of Western civilisation. To the uninitiated, Italian drivers may seem impatient and dangerous, with an over fondness for using their horns. However, most of them are highly skilful – they have to be – and are proud of their reflexes. Two attitudes to avoid are recklessness and excessive caution. Don't try to match their improvisations, you will only raise their competitive spirit into the realm of high risk. They may be similarly provoked by indecisive and slow drivers.

Keep your car for use on the open road. In cities, where scooters are an additional traffic hazard, the best option is to drop your bags off at the hotel and then park your car.

To see the city, the best way is often to walk, take a bus, an underground train or taxi, or rent a bike. Most towns have solved the problem for you by closing off their historical centres *(centro storico)* to traffic. A rental car will cost you money and remain unused.

Try to vary the kind of accommodation in which you choose to stay. Italy has all types available, so you'll have

Scooters are a favourite way of getting around town

quite a few choices. Small family-run hostelries and country inns are charming, but you should also consider indulging yourself for at least one night in the special comforts and pampering of the great hotels. Look for converted monasteries and countryside farmhouses, part of the very popular *agriturismo*. In most cases the frugality has long gone, the heating is modern and the medieval well has been replaced by a swimming pool, but the setting is still memorable.

Language Barrier

Even if you're linguistically challenged, try to learn a handful of words or expressions. The pronunciation is remarkably easy and Italians are usually delighted by anyone who makes the effort to speak their language. A cheerful *buon giorno* (good day) or *buona sera* (good evening) can work wonders when entering or leaving a shop or restaurant.

In a land where politeness is important, *per favore* (please), *grazie* (thank you), *prego* (don't mention it) and, when pushing through a bus or market, *permesso* (excuse me) will be greatly appreciated. You'll find some additional phrases in the Handy Travel Tips section, on page 222. *Buon viaggio!*

CENTRAL ITALY

The centre of Italy is the cradle of Latin civilisation, one-time administrative headquarters of that ancient conglomerate known as the Roman Empire. Immediately surrounding Rome, today's Lazio is the ancient province of Latium. On the eastern flank of the Apennines, the Abruzzi region, of which the province of Molise is a recently created offshoot, came under Roman domination in the 3rd century BC. First-time visitors will want to spend most or all of their time in Rome, but the area surrounding the capital makes a pleasant excursion. The rugged island of Sardinia deserves at least a week to do it justice, but you may want to spend a long weekend at one of its attractive seaside resorts.

Rome

Crowning seven hills along the winding banks of the River Tiber, Rome has numerous personalities: ancient Rome of imperial ruins; Catholic Rome of Vatican City and countless churches; the Renaissance city of Michelangelo and Raphael; the baroque of Bernini and Borromini. It is also a modern metropolis of interminable traffic jams, fashionable boutiques and cafés, as well as factories and characterless post-war suburbs. The secret of the Eternal City's magic is that it lives and relishes all its ages. Churches are built on the ruins of Roman baths or pagan temples; the trendy café crowd on Piazza Navona draw natural inspiration from Bernini's grandiose 17th-century fountain.

Ease yourself into this great city that has hosted visitors for millennia. To know its every nook and cranny is daunting, but by concentrating on the ancient city around the **Colosseum** or the **Vatican**, you will come to know one age at a time.

The Centre

Make an early start with breakfast (or come back for a late afternoon cooling drink) on **Piazza del Popolo** at **Caffè Rosati**, (Piazza del Popolo 4/5; open 7am–11.30pm), a glamorous Roman institution and historical meeting-place of the city's literary personalities, including such luminaries as the late Pasolini. Its outdoor tables are a perfect vantage point for admiring the gracefully curving *piazza*, an exemplary piece of open-air urban theatre designed in 1816 by Napoleon's architect Giuseppe Valadier.

To the north side, the church of **Santa Maria del Popolo** (open Mon–Sat 7am–noon and 4–7pm; Sun 8am–1.30pm and 4.30–7.30pm) is important for Raphael's handsome Chigi Chapel, exquisite frescoes by Pinturicchio and two profoundly disturbing early 17th-century paintings executed by Caravaggio, the *Conversion of St Paul* and *Crucifixion of St Peter*, in the Cerasi Chapel to the left of the main altar.

The Colosseum

Next to the church, an arched 16th-century gateway marks what was the entrance to ancient and medieval Rome along the Via Flaminia, leading from Rimini on the Adriatic coast. The **obelisk** in the *piazza*'s centre, dating from the Egypt of Ramesses II (13th century BC), was brought here from the Circus Maximus and re-erected by Pope Sixtus V in 1589. Rounding off the south side are the twin baroque churches, **Santa Maria dei Miracoli** and **Santa Maria in Montesanto**, completed by 17th-century masters Gianlorenzo Bernini and Carlo Fontana.

Above the piazza to the east, the **Pincio** Gardens (close at sunset) offer a magical view of the city. *(For the great art museum in Villa Borghese behind the Pincio, see page 67.)* The ascending Pincio promenade lined with umbrella pines takes you past **Villa Medici**, home of many French artists visiting on national

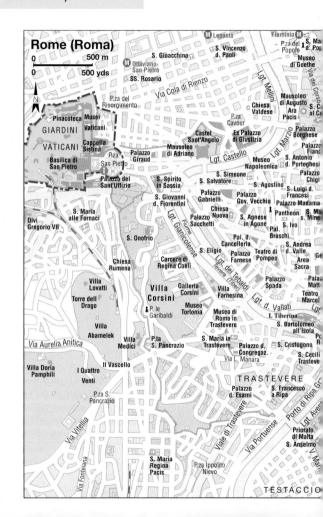

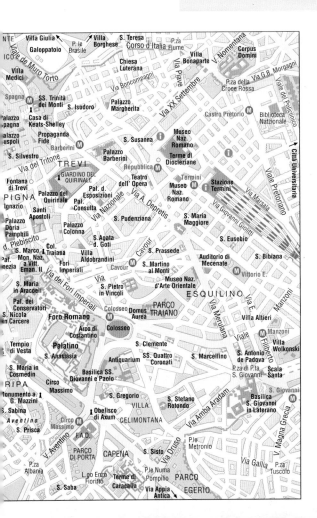

scholarships, to the 16th-century French church, **Trinità dei Monti**. Its twin belfries loom òver the **Spanish Steps** (*Scalinata della Trinità dei Monti*), eternal hang-out of Rome's golden youths, lovers, peddlers of trinkets and the occasional hustler. The pleasant daze induced on the three-tiered travertine staircase, festooned in spring with pink azaleas, was celebrated by John Keats as a 'blissful cloud of summer indolence' before he died here in 1821. His house at 26 Piazza di Spagna at the bottom of the steps has been preserved as a museum (open Mon–Fri 9am–1pm and 3–6pm; Sat 11am–2pm and 3–6pm).

Named after a palace used as the Spanish Embassy, the steps and the **Piazza di Spagna** are the heart of the city's most fashionable and exclusive shopping enclave, leading to the Via del Corso.

The Spanish Steps

The *piazza*'s 17th-century fountain, Fontana della Barcaccia, is by Bernini's father. Babington's Tea Rooms nearby are a relic of the days when Romans called the *piazza* the 'English ghetto'. More quintessentially Roman, on nearby Via Condotti, is the city's oldest coffee house, the 18th-century Caffè Greco – popular, as you'll see from pictures, busts and autographs, with Liszt, Baudelaire, Byron, Goethe, Casanova and Fellini.

This is the general area of the **Trevi Fountain** (*Fontana di Trevi*), which benefited from Fellini's keen sense of baroque aesthetics when he dipped the dazzling Anita Ekberg in its legendarily purifying waters for his 1960 film *La Dolce Vita*.

It's been quite some time since anyone was caught romping in these waters, which reflect Nicola Salvi's 18th- century fountain. Anyone caught frolicking in the water is liable to a hefty fine. The fountain is, in fact, a triumphal arch and palace façade (to the old Palazzo Poli) framing mythical creatures in a riot of rocks and pools, with a rearing horse symbolising the ocean's turmoil and a calmer steed its tranquillity.

Neptune at the Trevi Fountain

Tucked away behind alleys, this extravaganza is out of all proportion to its tiny *piazza,* and no amount of signposts leading to it can prepare you for the shock of discovery. Romantics go at the dead of night, to be alone with its illumination; it's also a favourite haunt for local fellows looking for foreign innocents abroad. Throw two coins over your shoulder into the fountain: the first is for a wish, the second to ensure that one day you will return. Coins are collected and given to Caritas, an Italian charity.

That other symbol of *la dolce vita,* the **Via Veneto**, has been deserted by its starlets and *paparazzi (*derived from Paparazzo, a news photographer in Fellini's *La Dolce Vita)* and only the expensive cafés, stylish shops and five-star hotels remain. Slowly, it is making something of a comeback in popularity.

Papal Residence

On one of the seven hills of ancient Rome, the fortress-like **Palazzo del Quirinale** (open Sun only 8.30am–12.30pm), once summer residence to popes fleeing the malarial swamps of the Vatican down by the Tiber, housed the new king of Italy after 1870 and, since 1947 has been the presidential palace. The only embellishment on its formidable façade is Bernini's graceful porch, but its *piazza* is worth the climb for the view over the city and the Vatican.

The giant marble monument to Vittorio Emanuele

You couldn't miss **Piazza Venezia** if you tried – and many do try, because of its endless traffic jams and the overpowering, ungainly white marble **Vittorio Emanuele Monument**. The monument, known familiarly as the 'Wedding Cake', celebrates the first king of unified Italy, as well as the Tomb of the Unknown Soldier, with inimitable 19th-century pomposity

Northwest of the monument, the 15th-century **Palazzo Venezia** (open Tues–Sat 8.30am–7pm) is a fine example of severe but elegant early Renaissance architecture, now home to a museum of medieval and Renaissance arms, furniture and sculpture. Mussolini had his office here and spoke to his followers from the balcony.

The Capitoline Hill
Beside the Piazza Venezia, a steep staircase leads up to the austere 13th-century **Santa Maria in Aracoeli,** while another, more graceful and gradual, takes you up between the statues of Castor and Pollux to Michelangelo's beautifully proportioned square of the **Campidoglio** (Capitoline Hill). This quiet traffic-free haven forges a superb link between the Renaissance and ancient

Rome's most sacred site, where sacrifices were made to Jupiter and Juno. The grand bronze equestrian **statue of Marcus Aurelius** that anchors the *piazza*'s centre is a copy; the restored original from the 2nd century AD is sheltered within the **Palazzo Nuovo** museum to its left. Opposite stands the **Palazzo dei Conservatori** and at the rear of the square is the handsome 16th-century façade of **Palazzo Senatorio** (now the City Hall). These two palaces house the Capitoline museums *(see page 67)*, whose Greek and Roman collections provide an excellent introduction to the ancient Roman Forum that spreads below it.

The church of **Il Gesù**, (open daily 6am–12.30pm and 4–7.15pm), severe and relatively discreet on its own square west of the Piazza Venezia, was a major element in the Jesuits' Counter-Reformation campaign. Begun as their Roman 'headquarters' in 1568, its open ground plan was the model for the Congregational churches that were to regain popular support from the Protestant faith. While its façade is more sober than the exultant baroque churches put up as the movement gained momentum, the interior glorifies the new militancy in gleaming bronze, gold,

The Wedding Cake

Few edifices have known such universal hostility as the Vittorio Emanuele Monument, or 'Vittoriano'. Popularly known as the 'Wedding Cake' or 'Rome's False Teeth', the bombastic colonnade with its equestrian bronzes and almost unscaleable steps are a true monument of urban catastrophe. Begun in 1885, the 40-year construction entailed the demolition of a piece of the ancient Capitoline Hill. Parts of the Palazzo Venezia were dismantled for a clearer view. The gigantic proportions completely dwarf the surrounding splendours of ancient Rome and the dazzling white Brescia marble clashes with the city's preference for gentle amber, ochre or pink travertine. In 1944, art historians were said to have pleaded with the Allies to suspend Rome's status as an open city – protecting it against bombardment – just long enough to destroy the Vittoriano.

Inside St Ignatius Loyola

marble and precious stones. Inevitably, the most elaborate ornament is the **altar of St Ignatius Loyola** (Sant'Ignazio), covering the tomb of the Jesuits' Spanish founder in the left transept. Its profusion of lapis lazuli is actually a thin shell fused to plaster stucco.

In gentle contrast, the nearby church of **Sant'Ignazio** stands in an enchanting rococo stage-set of 17th-century houses. Inside, Andrea Pozzo (a Jesuit priest and designer of the saint's tomb at Gesù church) painted a superb *trompe l'oeil* ceiling fresco (1685) depicting St Ignatius' entry into paradise.

Temple of the Gods

The circular **Pantheon** (Piazza della Rotonda; open Mon–Sat 9am–6pm, Sun 9am–1pm except during mass at 10.30am) is the best-preserved monument of ancient Rome and rivals the Colosseum in its combination of quiet elegance and massive power. Built by Emperor Hadrian around AD120 on an earlier site destroyed by fire, it achieved a marvel of engineering with its magnificent coffered dome: over 43m (141ft) in interior diameter (larger than St Peter's), exactly equal to its height. Bronze that once embellished the entrance was carted away and recycled as Bernini's canopy for the high altar in St Peter's. This 'Temple of all the Gods' today contains the tombs of Renaissance masters such as Raphael, as well as the first king of Italy, Vittorio Emanuele II, and his son Umberto I.

Some of Caravaggio's greatest masterpieces are in the neighbourhood: the *St Matthew* trilogy (1597–1602) in the fine baroque church of **San Luigi dei Francesi** and the moving *Madonna of the Pilgrims* (1609) in the Renaissance church of **Sant'Agostino**.

Pause a moment at a café in that most serene of city squares: nowhere in Rome is the spectacle of Italian street life more pleasantly indulged than in the **Piazza Navona**, thanks to an inspired collaboration of Roman genius across the ages. The elongated oval *piazza* was laid out around AD79 by Emperor Domitian as an athletics stadium, *Circus Agonalis* – a sporting tradition that was continued in the Middle Ages with jousting tournaments and with other events in the centuries that followed. The 17th century contributed its sublime baroque décor and today it is protected as Rome's most beloved square. In the centre, Bernini's **Fountain of the Four Rivers** *(Fontana dei Fiumi)* celebrates the great rivers of the four continents: the Americas (Río de la Plata), Europe (Danube), Asia (Ganges) and Africa (Nile). Romans who delight in Bernini's scorn for his rivals suggest that the Nile god covers his head rather than look at Borromini's church of **Sant'Agnese in Agone**, and the river god of the Americas is poised to catch it in case it collapses. In fact, the fountain was completed several years *before* Borromini's structurally impeccable façade and dome.

The Pantheon interior

A large and boisterous fruit, vegetable and flower market takes place in the mornings (Mon–Sat 8am–1pm), in the **Campo de' Fiori**, overseen by the statue of philosopher Giordano Bruno. The Counter Reformation burnt him alive here in 1600 for his preposterous idea that the universe was infinite, with many more galaxies than ours. An even more famous death occurred at the nearby Piazza del Biscione, more precisely the restaurant Da Pancrazio (tel: 06 686 1246) at No. 92, whose cellar shelters ruins of Pompeii's Theatre where Julius Caesar was assassinated.

Although generally closed to the public, the glorious **Palazzo Farnese**, built by Antonio da Sangallo the Younger, Michelangelo and Giacomo della Porta from 1514, now houses the French Embassy. Only the inner courtyard of Rome's finest Renaissance palace is accessible to the public, but its grand portico and the handsome stuccoed vestibule leading to it make it well worth a visit. Narrow streets southeast of the Campo dei Fiori take you to the **Jewish Ghetto** near the ruins of the ancient Roman Theatre of Marcellus *(Teatro di Marcello)*, architectural model for the Colosseum. Jews have been a permanent feature of Roman life for over 2,500 years but were forced into a ghetto in the 16th century. A small Jewish community is still based nearby around the Via del Portico d'Ottavia. The hefty neo-Babylonian synagogue (inaugurated in 1904), with a small museum of Jewish history next door, is by the river bank.

Classical Rome

The nucleus of classical Rome is around the Colosseum, with the Forum to the northwest and the Baths of Caracalla to the south. Don't be daunted – even the best-informed scholars find the monumental relics difficult to decipher – the mystery itself is more than half the charm of these vestiges of a vanished world. Take them in your stride, avoid the midday sun in the shadeless Forum and finish your visit with a picnic and *siesta* on the Palatine. Even if you're not an archaeology buff who wants to understand the meaning of every stone, it's worth at least an hour or two to stand among the débris of an empire and wonder whether Fifth Avenue, Piccadilly, the Champs-Elysées or Red Square will look any better 2,000 years from now.

Of Rome's countless inspirational churches, *palazzi* and monuments, it is the **Colosseum** (open daily Mar–Oct 9am–6.15pm; or one hour before sunset, Nov–Feb 9am–4.30pm; times may

The 'gladiators' bloody circus' seated over 50,000

vary) that is the symbol of the city's eternity. The building that Lord Byron called 'the gladiator's bloody circus' was started by the emperor Vespasian, founder of the Republic, in AD72; the four-tiered elliptical amphitheatre seated more than 50,000 spectators. Flowing in and out of 80 arched passageways known as *vomitoria*, aristocrats and plebians came to see blood: bears, lions, tigers, leopards and other exotic, wild beasts were starved into fighting each other and against criminals, war captives and (according to some historians) Christians. Gladiators, once criminals and slaves but later professional warriors, fought one another to the crowds' cries of *Jugula!* ('Slit his throat!')

For their churches and private palaces, popes and princes have stripped the Colosseum of its precious marble, travertine and metal. In the arena's basin, they have left a ruined maze of cells and corridors that funnelled men and beasts to the slaughter. The horror has disappeared beneath the moss and what remains is the thrill of the monument's endurance. In his *Childe Harold's Pilgrimage* (1812–18), Byron wrote: 'While stands the Colosseum, Rome shall stand; when falls the Colosseum, Rome shall fall; and

The Forum, hub of ancient Rome

when Rome falls, with it shall fall the world.' There is reason to believe it shall stand forever, a massive top-to-toe restoration completed in 1999 has it looking rejuvenated and soot-free.

The nearby **Arch of Constantine** celebrates the 4th-century emperor's battlefield conversion to Christianity. A frugal Senate took a number of fragments from monuments of earlier rulers Trajan, Hadrian and Marcus Aurelius in order to decorate the arch.

Northeast of the Colosseum is the **Domus Aurea**, a fabulous villa built by the Emperor Nero, who spent just a few years in his 'Golden House' (the façade was clad in solid gold) before killing himself in AD68. On a site once 25 times the size of the Colosseum, 30 of the 250 rooms in the palace can be visited by guided tour only with a maximum of 10 people at a time (open Wed–Mon 9am–7.45pm; tel: 06 3996 7700; <www.pierreci.it>). Note that the temperature is a constant 10°C (50°F), so wear something warm.

The Roman Forum

With an exhilarating leap of the imagination, you can stand among the columns, arches and porticoes of the **Roman Forum** (open daily 9am–6.15pm in summer, 9am–4.30pm in winter; last entry one hour before closing) and picture the civic, commercial and religious hub of the great city, the first in Europe to house a million inhabitants. Earthquake, fire, flood and the plunder of barbarians and Renaissance architects reduced the area to a muddy cow pasture until the excavations of the 19th century. Today, a detailed map and portable sound-guides rented at the entrance (on the Via dei Fori Imperiali) will make sense of the apparent confusion and help you trace the layout of palaces, temples and market halls.

Part of the brick-built **Curia**, home of the Roman Senate, still stands. Steps nearby lead underground to the **Lapis Niger**, a black marble pavement laid by Julius Caesar over the presumed grave of Romulus, the city's founder. To the south of it are remains of the Basilica Julia law court and the **Rostra** orators' platform from which Mark Antony informed the people of Caesar's assassination. Countless Renaissance and baroque sculptors have drawn inspiration from the friezes on the triple **Arch of Septimius Severus** (a 3rd-century emperor who died in York, England, the northernmost boundary of the empire).

The **Temple of Saturn** doubled as state treasury and centre of the December debauchery known as the Saturnalia, pagan precursor of Christmas. In the circular **Temple of Vesta**, the sacred flame perpetuating the Roman state was tended by six Vestal Virgins who, from childhood, observed a 30-year vow of chastity on fear of being buried alive if they broke it. At the end of the Via Sacra, the **Arch of Titus** commemorates the sacking of Jerusalem in AD70.

The most impressive monument of the Imperial Forums, built as an adjunct to the Roman Forum in honour of Julius Caesar, Augustus,

Lost in the Classical world

Trajan, Vespasian and Domitian, is the 30-m (100-ft) **Trajan's Column** (AD113). Celebrating Trajan's campaigns against the Dacians in what is now Romania, the detailed friezes spiralling around the column constitute a textbook of Roman warfare. St Peter's statue on top replaced that of the emperor's in 1587.

South of the Forum, a slope leads up to the **Palatine Hill** (open daily 9am–6.15pm, until 4.30pm Nov–Mar; last entry one hour before closing), the legendary birthplace of Rome, the history of which is charted by the **Palatine Museum** (open daily 9am–6.15pm, until 4.30pm Nov–Mar; last entry one hour before closing), now open after 13 years' restoration. Today the hill is a romantic garden, dotted with toppled columns among the wild flowers and spiny acanthus shrubs. Only rows of cypress trees and pavilions remain from the botanical gardens laid out here in the 16th century. From its grassy knolls, enjoy the fine view back over the Colosseum or southwards over the **Circus Maximus**, where chariot races were held for huge crowds of up to 200,000.

Trajan's Column

Just 1km (⅔ mile) south of the Colosseum, the 3rd-century **Baths of Caracalla** (*Terme di Caracalla*; open summer Tues–Sat 9am–6.30pm and Mon and Sun 9am–1pm; winter Tues–Sat 9am–3pm and Mon and Sun 9am–1pm) were built for 1,600 people to bathe in style and luxury. The baths and gymnasia were of alabaster and granite, decorated with statues and frescoes. Public bathing used to be a prolonged social event, as merchants and senators passed from the *calidarium* (hot room) to cool down in the *tepidarium* and *frigidarium*.

South of the baths begins the **Old Appian Way** *(Via Appia Antica)*, built in 312BC for the Roman legions who marched to coastal Brindisi to set sail for the Levant and North Africa. On either side lie the ruins of sepulchres of 20 generations of patrician families. The 17th-

The Baths of Caracalla

century chapel of Domine Quo Vadis marks the site where St Peter, fleeing Nero's persecution in Rome, is said to have encountered Christ. Further along the Via Appia are three of Rome's most celebrated catacombs, including those of **St Callisto** (open Thur–Tues 8.30am–noon and 2.30pm–5.30pm; closed early Oct–Mar), the largest of some 50 underground Christian cemeteries.

The Vatican

The power of Rome endures both in the spirituality evoked by every stone of St Peter's Basilica and in the almost physical awe inspired by the splendours of **Vatican City**. At their best, the popes and cardinals replaced military conquest by moral leadership and persuasion; at their worst, they could show the same hunger for political power and worldly wealth as any Caesar or grand duke. A visit to the Vatican is an object lesson for faithful and sceptic alike (Vatican Tourist Office, Piazza San Pietro, tel: 06 6988 1662; open Mon–Sat 8.30am–7pm, last entry at 6.30pm; for general information about St Peter's and the Vatican; <www. vatican.va>).

Named after the hill on which it stands and which in the Middle Ages was surrounded by a malarial swamp, the Vatican has been a papal residence for over 600 years, but a sovereign state independent of Italy only since the Lateran Treaty signed by Mussolini in

Castel Sant'Angelo

1929. It is preferable to visit St Peter's Basilica and the Vatican Museums on separate days to avoid fatigue and visual overload. Check with the tourist office for opening times, as they are liable to change.

To appreciate the unique panorama of St Peter's Basilica and its 1 sq km (⅔ sq mile) *piazza*, approach it by foot as history's countless pilgrims have done. Cross at the beautiful **Sant'Angelo Bridge**, one of 20 crossing the Tiber River. Adorned by ten angel sculptures by Bernini and his studio, it arrives at the **Castel Sant'Angelo** (open Tues–Sun 9am–8pm), originally built as Hadrian's mausoleum in AD139. Its name derives from Pope Gregory's vision of the Archangel Michael – now represented by a statue on top – heralding the end of a plague in 590. Sixth-century barbarians commandeered the round, brick pile as a fortress, using ancient statues as missiles to hurl onto their enemies below. Linked to the Vatican by a thick-walled passage, it served as a hideout for popes in times of danger, notably for Pope Clement VII, holed up here for a month during the sack of Rome by Habsburg troops in 1527 *(see page 26)*. The Papal Apartments are a contrast to the dungeons, both open to the public, where philosopher and monk Giordano Bruno and sculptor-goldsmith Benvenuto Cellini were imprisoned.

St Peter's

In **St Peter's Square** *(Piazza San Pietro)*, Bernini has performed one of the world's most exciting pieces of architectural orchestration. The sweeping curves of the colonnades reach out to the unending stream of pilgrims from Rome and the whole world, *urbi et orbi*, to take them into the bosom of the church beyond.

Bernini completed the 284 travertine columns, 88 pilasters and 140 statues of the saints in just 11 years, in 1667. Stand on either of the circular paving stones set between the square's twin 17th-century fountains and the red granite Egyptian obelisk to appreciate the harmony of the quadruple rows of Doric columns, so perfectly aligned that they seem like a single row.

St Peter's Basilica (open daily Apr–Sept 7am–7pm; Oct– Mar 7am–6pm) is the largest of all Roman Catholic churches and by any standards a grandiose achievement, but it suffered from the competing visions of all the architects called in to collaborate – Bramante, Giuliano da Sangallo, Raphael, Baldassare Peruzzi, Michelangelo, Giacomo Della Porta, Domenico Fontana and Carlo Maderno. From 1506 to 1626, it changed from the simple ground plan of a Greek cross, with four arms of equal length, as favoured by Bramante and his arch-enemy Michelangelo, to the final form of Maderno's Latin cross extended by a long nave, as demanded by the popes of the Counter-Reformation. One result

The view from St Peter's

An incomparable array of treasures at the Vatican Museum

is that Maderno's porticoed façade and nave obstruct a clear view of Michelangelo's dome from the square.

The church's dimensions are impressive: 212m (695ft) exterior length, 187m (613ft) inside length; 132m (435ft) to the tip of the dome (diameter 42.45m/139ft). As you go in, note St Peter's keys inlaid in the doorway paving. Set in the floor by the central door is the large round slab of red porphyry where Charlemagne knelt for his coronation as the first Holy Roman Emperor in AD800.

You'll find the basilica's most treasured work of art, Michelangelo's sublime **Pietà** – Mary with the dead Jesus on her lap – in its own chapel to the right of the entrance. The Florentine artist was 25 and justly proud enough to append his signature (the only surviving example), visible on the Madonna's sash. Since a religious fanatic attacked it with a hammer in 1972, the statue has been protected by bullet-proof glass. But reverence can also cause damage: on the 13th-century bronze **statue of St Peter** near the main altar, attributed to Florentine architect-sculptor Arnolfo di Cambio, the lips and fingers of countless pilgrims have worn away the toes of its right foot.

Beneath the dome, Bernini's great **baldacchino** (canopy), cast out of bronze beams taken from the Pantheon's porch *(see page 52)*, soars above the high altar. It was built right over St Peter's tomb and reserved exclusively for the pope's Mass. In the apse beyond, the baroque master gives full vent to his exuberance with his bronze and marble **Cathedra of St Peter**, throne of the Apostle's successors.

Vatican Treasures

The greatest patron that painters, sculptors and architects have ever known, the Catholic Church, houses in its headquarters, one of the richest collections of art in the world. The 7 km (4 miles) of rooms and galleries of the **Vatican Museums** (*Musei Vaticani*; open mid-Mar–late-Oct Mon–Fri 8.45am–4.45pm, Sat 8.45am–1.45pm; Nov–mid-Mar Mon–Sat 8.45am–1.45pm; last entry 1 hour 25 mins before closing; open last Sun of month 9am–1pm year-round) are made up of eight museums, five galleries, the Apostolic Library, the Borgia Apartments, the Raphael Stanze (or Rooms) and the incomparable Sistine Chapel. Shuttle buses run regularly from St Peter's Square to the

Meeting the Pope

When he's not abroad on official foreign visits it may be possible to see Pope Benedict XVI in person at the Vatican. He holds a public audience every Wednesday at 11am (5pm in summer) in the Papal Audience Hall. Tickets may be obtained from the Pontifical Prefect's Office (open 9am–1pm; tel: 6988 4631. Apply on the Tuesday before the audience) through the bronze gates in St Peter's Square. A visitor's bishop at home can arrange a private audience. On Sundays at noon, the pope appears at the window of his apartments in the Apostolic Palace (right of the basilica, overlooking the square), delivers a brief homily, says the Angelus and blesses the crowd below. On a few major holy days, the pontiff celebrates high Mass in St Peter's. Note the very strict dress code (no shorts, uncovered shoulders or bare midriffs).

museum entrance and back, which otherwise would be a 20-minute walk.

If you want at all costs to avoid the Sistine's day-long crowds, go there first thing in the morning (don't forget your binoculars for details on the ceiling). In any case, you can't miss it – arrows indicate colour-coded itineraries within the museum that showcase the myriad marvels to see en route, a remarkable degree of which is overlooked by time-restricted visitors on a mission.

With the booty from the ruthless dismantling of ancient monuments to make way for the Renaissance city in the 16th century, the **Pio-Clementino Museum** has assembled a wonderful collection of Roman and Greek art. Most celebrated is the tortured *Laocoön* group from Rhodes.

Pope Julius II took a risk in 1508 when he called in a relatively untried 26-year-old to do the interior decoration of his new apartments. The result was the four **Raphael Rooms** *(Stanze di Raffaello)*. In the central Stanza della Segnatura are the two masterly frescoes, *Dispute over the Holy Sacrament* and the famous *School of Athens*, confronting theological with philosophical wisdom.

In stark contrast to Raphael's grand manner, seek out the gentle beauty of Fra Angelico's frescoes in the **Chapel of Nicholas V** *(Cappella del Beato Angelico)*. The lives of Saints Lawrence and Stephen are depicted in subdued pinks and blues.

The lavishly decorated **Borgia Apartments** contain Pinturicchio's frescoes with portraits of the Spanish Borgia Pope Alexander VI and his notorious son Cesare and daughter Lucrezia and leads into the collection of modern religious artwork opened in 1973 by Paul VI. The latter includes Rodin bronzes, Picasso ceramics, Matisse's Madonna sketches and designs for ecclesiastical robes and, rather unexpectedly, a grotesque Francis Bacon pope.

> The Sistine Chapel was sculptor Michelangelo's first fresco painting. After Pope Julius II threatened to throw him off the scaffolding if he didn't hurry up, he wrote to a friend: 'I am not in a good place, and I am no painter.'

The Sistine Chapel

Nothing can prepare you for the visual feast of the **Sistine Chapel** (*Cappella Sistina*; ticket office open Easter–Oct Mon–Fri 8.45am–3.20pm, last exit 4.45pm; Sat 8.45pm–12.20pm, last exit 1.45pm; closed Sun except fourth Sun in month when admission is free; in winter, open on same days as above, but 8.45am–12.20pm only), built for Sixtus IV in the 15th century. Restored to its original colours after restoration over the past two decades, the fresco is overwhelming. Despite the distraction of the constant crowds (quiet is requested), visitors seem to yield to the power of

The Sistine Chapel ceiling

Michelangelo's ceiling and his *Last Judgement*. The other wall frescoes by Botticelli, Pinturicchio, Ghirlandaio and Signorelli are barely given attention. In this private papal chapel, where cardinals hold their conclave to elect a new pope, the glory of the Catholic Church achieves its finest artistic expression.

The chapel portrays nothing less than the story of man, in three parts: from Adam to Noah; the giving of the Law to Moses; and from the birth of Jesus to the Last Judgment. Towards the centre of Michelangelo's **ceiling**, you'll make out the celebrated outstretched finger of man's creation, filled out by the drunkenness of Noah, the turmoil of the Flood. But most overwhelming of all is the impression of the whole – best appreciated looking back from the bench by the chapel's exit.

On the chapel's altar wall is Michelangelo's tempestuous **Last Judgment**, begun 23 years after the ceiling's completion

At Trastevere Flea Market

in 1512, when he was 60 and imbued with religious soul-searching. It is said that the artist's agonising self-portrait can be made out in the flayed skin of St Bartholomew, to the right below Jesus.

Amid all the Vatican's treasures, the 15 rooms of the **Picture Gallery** *(Pinacoteca Vaticana)*, located in a separate wing of the palace, get short shrift. This collection of nine centuries of paintings includes works by Giotto, Fra Angelico, Perugino, Raphael's *Transfiguration* (his last great work), Leonardo da Vinci's unfinished *St Jerome*, Bellini's *Pietà* and Caravaggio's *Descent from the Cross*.

Trastevere

The neighbourhood south of the Vatican, **Trastevere**, literally 'across the Tiber', has long been renowned as the most popular quarter of Rome. Here, ordinary people who consider themselves the original citizens of the city uphold age-old traditions and customs (much like the Cockneys in London). It is good to wander among the narrow streets and markets to sample the authentic life of the city, highlighted by the *Noantri* ('We Others') street festival of music, food and fireworks, in the last two weeks of July. Another sort of festival atmosphere prevails every Sunday, when the Porta Portese section of Trastevere hosts Rome's liveliest and largest flea market.

Inevitably, 'popular' and 'authentic' became chic and the ambience is now somewhat contested by higher rents. But the true Trasteverini hang on, mainly in the area immediately around **Santa Maria in Trastevere**, reputedly the oldest church in the city. Its foundation may date back to the 3rd century, but the present structure is the work of Pope Innocent II, himself a Trasteverino, around 1140. It's known for its wonderful Byzantine-influenced façade and interior pavements and **mosaic** apse ceiling of Mary enthroned with Jesus.

Other Museums

The largest collection of Etruscan art in Italy can be found in the 16th-century **Villa Giulia** (open Tues–Sun 8.30am–7pm, last entry 6.30pm) in the northwest area of the Villa Borghese park. Room after room is filled with objects from the tombs of this little understood pre-Roman people. The **Borghese Gallery** (open Tues–Sun 9am–7pm; tickets must be booked in advance for obligatory tours, tel: 06 32810, <www.ticketeria.it>, ticket office closes 6.30pm) is housed in a baroque villa inspired by Hadrian's Villa at Tivoli *(see page 70)*, but with Italian for-

The Borghese Gallery

mal gardens transformed into an English-style landscaped park. One of Italy's loveliest and most important small museums, its highlights include sculptures by Bernini and Canova (whose portrayal of Napoleon's sister as a reclining Venus is famous), and paintings by Botticelli, Caravaggio, Correggio, Cranach, Dürer, Raphael, Rubens and Titian.

The Villa is home to Italy's most important Etruscan museum, the **Museo Nazionale Etrusco**. The collection includes finds from major excavations in Lazio and Tuscany, countless Etruscan artefacts and a reconstructed Etruscan temple.

The **Capitoline Museums** (open Tues–Sun 9am–8pm,

The Capitoline She-Wolf

ticket office closes one hour earlier; <www.museicapitolini.org>), in the twin palaces of the Campidoglio *(see page 50)*, have extensive collections of sculpture excavated from ancient Rome, particularly in the Palazzo Nuovo. In the Palazzo dei Conservatori is the most celebrated piece, the superb Etruscan bronze **Capitoline She-Wolf** *(Lupa Capitolina)*, symbol of the city. The wolf dates from around the 5th century BC, but the Romulus and Remus are Renaissance additions by Pollaiuolo. The top-floor **Capitoline Picture Gallery** *(Pinacoteca Capitolina)* has works by Bellini, Titian, Tintoretto, Lotto and Veronese, Rubens and Caravaggio.

On the Via delle Quattro Fontane is the **Palazzo Barberini**, also known as the **National Gallery of Antique Art** *(Galleria Nazionale d'Arte Antica*; open Tues–Sun 9am– 7pm; till 10pm on some Fri and Sat). This is another architectural battleground for rivals Borromini and Bernini, worth a visit as much for its baroque décor as for its collection of 13th- to 17th-century paintings.

Palazzo Doria Pamphilj (gallery open Fri–Wed 10am–5pm) off Piazza Venezia. Now one of Rome's top museums, this rococo palace houses over 400 paintings, representing one of the city's most important private late Renaissance collections. The family's private apartments are exquisitely furnished, and the picture gallery includes masterpieces such as Titian's *Salome with the head of St John* and Caravaggio's *St John the Baptist*. There is also a fine collection of Dutch and Flemish works.

Other Churches

It's impossible to even count all of the churches worth visiting in Rome (unofficial counts hover at 250). We suggest three within easy reach of the Via Cavour en route from Stazione Termini.

Built in the 4th century on the Esquiline Hill site of a Roman temple to the goddess Juno is the largest and most splendid of the churches dedicated to the Virgin, **Santa Maria Maggiore** (open daily 7am–7pm). Christmas is especially popular here when pilgrims come to admire relics of the holy crib from Bethlehem. The most spectacular art treasures of the church are its Byzantine mosaics, shimmering Old Testament scenes high on the walls (don't forget the binoculars) and a triumphant Mary and Jesus enthroned in the apse over the high altar. The coffered Renaissance ceiling glitters with the gold of the first shipments from the New World.

In a nearby side street, **Santa Prassede** (open daily 7am– noon and 4–6.30pm) is unprepossessing from the outside but enchanting in the intimacy of its interior. The richly coloured 9th-century Byzantine mosaics of Jesus and four angels make the Chapel of St Zeno the city's most important Byzantine monument. To the right of the chapel is a fragment of rare jasper said to come from the column to which Jesus was tied for his flagellation.

San Pietro in Vincoli (St Peter in Chains; open daily 7am– 12.30pm and 3.30–7pm) might not attract a second look if it didn't contain one of the greatest of Michelangelo's sculptures, his formidable *Moses* (1515). It was intended for St Peter's Basilica as part of Michelangelo's lavish (but botched) project for Pope Julius II's tomb – Moses was supposed to be one of 40 figures adorning the tomb. On each side, the comparatively passive figures of Jacob's wives, a prayerful Rachel and melancholy Leah, were the last completed sculptures of Michelangelo. In the *Reliquary* are St Peter's chains, which, according to tradition, shackled him while he was held in the Mamertine Prison.

Santa Maria Maggiore

Lazio

The excursions to be made today into the Lazio hinterland around Rome are those that ancient Romans themselves made to holiday homes by the sea or nearby lakes.

Tivoli

Follow the old Roman chariot road (re-paved) of Via Tiburtina 30 km (19 miles) east of the capital to the haunting ruins of **Hadrian's Villa** (*Villa Adriana*; open daily 9am–one hour before sunset, till 3.30pm in winter), situated near the picturesque town of **Tivoli**, at the foot of the Sabine Hills. Sprawling across 70 hectares (173 acres), this retirement hideaway of the great emperor-builder was designed to recapture some of the architectural marvels of his empire. Barbarians and museum curators have removed that majority of the villa's treasures, but a stroll through the remaining pillars, arches and mosaic fragments in gardens running wild among the olive trees, cypresses and pines can be marvellously evocative of a lost world.

Hadrian's Villa

Located right in the centre is the delightful **Villa dell' Isola**. This pavilion, surrounded by a little reflecting pool and circular portico, epitomises the magic of the place.

Set in Tivoli itself, overlooking the Roman plain, the **Villa d'Este** (open Tues–Sun 8.30am–one hour before sunset), is a 16th-century counterpart that celebrates all the extravagance of the late Renaissance. From the home of Cardinal Ippolito d'Este, guests can survey the terraced gardens, the real reason for Tivoli's fame: alleys of cypresses and soaring fountains (including Bernini's *Bicchierone*), grottoes, waterfalls and pools. The hydraulic **Organ Fountain** plays at 10.30am, 12.30pm, 2.30pm, 4.30pm and 6.30pm. The **Fountain della Civetta** is active at 10am, noon, 2pm, 4pm and 6pm.

Alban Hills and Castel Gandolfo

The region southeast of Rome is known locally as the Castelli Romani (Roman Castles) for the fortified hilltop refuges built during the medieval civil wars. Today it's the summer heat that drives the Romans out on day-trips to the vineyards of the Alban hills and lakes. The country villages of **Frascati**, **Grottaferrata**, **Marino** and **Rocca di Papa** make delightful stops, not least for a cool glass of their white wine, especially during the autumn grape-harvest festivals. The pope's summer palace is at **Castel Gandolfo**, on the shores of Lake Albano – note that his Wednesday and Sunday blessings from mid-July to early September are not guaranteed.

Tarquinia and Northern Lazio

The A12 *autostrada* and the old Via Aurelia (which ends up in Arles in French Provence) take you to **Tarquinia**. Most important of the original 12 towns of the Etruscan confederation, it dominated Rome in its 6th- to 7th-century BC heyday. Today, the paintings and sculptures found in its **necropolis** of over 5,700 tombs provide evidence of the brilliant Etruscan civilisation. Visits to the tombs outside of town are organised from the **National Museum** (open Tues–Sun, summer 8.30am–7.30pm; winter 8.30am–4.30pm) in the fine 15th-century Gothic-Renaissance Palazzo Vitelleschi as you enter Tarquinia. The museum exhibits sarcophagi, Etruscan and imported Greek vases and some of the best wall paintings – all in reconstructed tombs.

Tuscania is a quiet little fortified town, shaken in 1971 by an earthquake that fortunately did not harm its two fine Romanesque churches, which are situated on the eastern outskirts (check with the tourist office on Piazza Basile for the churches' erratic opening hours).

In the restful charm of its medieval quarters, **Viterbo** makes a good overnight stop. The oldest neighbourhood, with narrow streets and little market squares, is around the Via San Pellegrino. On the equally attractive Piazza San Lorenzo, the Palazzo Papale has an impressive 13th-century Gothic loggia, opposite the Romanesque Cathedral with Renaissance façade.

Sardinia *(Sardegna)*

The Mediterranean's second-largest island (after Sicily) is well worth a holiday all to itself. Those curious to get a feel for its unique atmosphere should consider staying at small seaside resorts, combining meandering drives along Sardinia's coastline with excursions into the rugged hinterland. Prehistoric man dotted the island with mysterious cone-shaped *nuraghi* houses and watchtowers before it was then colonised by Cretans, Phoenicians, Carthaginians and Romans. Later, Sardinia became part of the commercial empires of Pisa, Genoa and Spain, and was annexed in 1718 by the dukes of Savoy – although malarial mosquitoes and repressive feudalism hindered development until the 19th century. The Costa Smeralda is popular with the European yachting set and celebrities, and in August hotels are booked up months in advance.

Costa Smeralda, Sardinia

Cagliari

The island's capital and main port is a largely modern city, but with a Spanish flavour to its older quarters up on the hill. The **Archaeological Museum** (open Tues–Sun 9am– 8pm) has important bronze statues of warriors and priests found in prehistoric tombs and artefacts from the Nuraghic culture. The much-renovated cathedral has two superbly carved 12th-cen-

Fishing nets

tury pulpits, commissioned for the cathedral in Pisa. Before heading for the open road, try the excellent local cuisine, including Spanish-style fish stews and Genoese pasta dishes.

The **Cagliari-Muravera** road winding across the plunging ravines of the Sarrabus mountains to the coast is one of the island's most spectacular drives. Continue then up the coast to Lanusei and head inland across the rugged **Gennargentu mountains**, covered with dense forests of cork oak and chestnut trees. Further north, just off the Nuoro-Dorgali road is the secluded site of **Serra Orrios**, a well-preserved prehistoric village (signposted *Villaggio Nuragico*). A short walk along a marked path through the fields takes you to a group of dry-stone houses with two temples and circular ramparts in a lovely setting of eucalyptus and olive trees. Archaeologists have located some 7,000 of these *nuraghi* structures around the island, believed to be parts of fortified citadels.

Costa Smeralda

The glittering **Costa Smeralda** on the northeast tip of the island is one of Italy's smartest resort areas, with beautiful beaches, five-star hotels, sports complexes and exclusive marinas for yachts and motor launches. It stretches around bays and rocky inlets from Olbia in the east to the promontory of La Maddalena. **Porto Cervo** is the coast's fashionable centre, but **Baia Sar-**

Castelsardo

dinia competes with its craggy coastline. More exclusive is the little luxury resort island and fishing village of **La Maddalena**, just a 15-minute ferry-ride from Palau. It is the principal island of an archipelago of 14, most of them little more than piles of rocks.

Linked to La Maddalena by a 7-km (4-mile) causeway, the isle of **Caprera** was the last home of Giuseppe Garibaldi, *(see page 30)* military leader of the Risorgimento movement for Italian unity. The house where he died in 1882 (his tomb is nearby) is now a museum.

The north coast road makes an enjoyable excursion along the dunes and pine groves lining the Gulf of Asinara. The fortress-town of **Castelsardo** stands high on a spectacular promontory overlooking the gulf. Inside its 16th-century cathedral, you can hear the sea crashing on the rocks directly below the foundations. At **Porto Torres** is the important 11th-century Pisan Romanesque church of San Gavino. Its interior is of a noble simplicity.

Alghero

This quiet little seaside resort on the northwest coast has a pleasant Catalan flavour to its older quarters around the cathedral. Take a sunset stroll along the 16th-century Spanish ramparts.

There's good fishing to be had in the nearby bay of Porto Conte and the Palmavera *nuraghi* citadel is well worth a visit. On the bay's southwestern promontory is the fascinating **Grotta di Nettuno** (Neptune's Grotto; open daily Apr–Sept 9am–8pm; Oct 10am–5pm, Nov–Mar 9am–3pm). Guided tours of these subterranean caverns with their dramatic stalactites and stalagmites are organised by boat from Alghero or on foot directly at the site, down a steep stairway in the cliffs.

TUSCANY AND UMBRIA

Light is the secret of Tuscany's magic. In that apparently miraculous collision of imagination and intellect that sparked the Renaissance in 15th-century Florence, its painters and architects had the constant inspiration of the dramatic changes in Tuscan light from dawn to dusk. And more than anywhere else in the country, Tuscany and neighbouring land-locked Umbria present the ideal green Italian landscape, dotted with stalwart hilltop towns, where cypress-tree sentinels watch over groves of twisted olive groves and vineyards blanket the gentle rolling hills.

Florence lies at the heart of the northern Apennines, in a basin of the Arno river which runs out to Pisa and the sea. Siena, its proud historic rival, dominates the Tuscan hill towns to the south, while the university towns of Perugia and Assisi are the keys to Umbria's luminous beauty. With some careful timing, modern visitors can capture a glimpse of that miracle of light. Arrive

Cypress trees and terracotta tiles in a typical Tuscany scene

early in the morning for your first look across the hills from the grey-stone towers of San Gimignano (a 'medieval Manhattan'), or visit Siena's Piazza del Campo at sunset. The dazzling white marble of Pisa's Duomo and leaning campanile is breathtaking in the noonday sun, but late afternoon is the blessed moment for the brilliant mosaic façade of Orvieto's cathedral.

Florence *(Firenze)*

Florence is one of the world's great tourist magnates and has architecture, history and artwork in quantities not found elsewhere in the world. Our itineraries divide the city's heart into four quarters: from the Duomo north to Piazza San Marco; from Piazza della Signoria, Palazzo Vecchio and the Uffizi Galleries east to Piazza Santa Croce; from the Mercato Nuovo west to Piazza Santa Maria Novella; and the southern 'Left Bank' of the Arno River around the Pitti Palace and Piazzale Michelangelo.

From the Duomo to Piazza San Marco

The **Duomo** (cathedral; open Mon–Sat 10am–5pm, till 3.30pm on Thur, Sun 1.30–4.45pm), officially Santa Maria del Fiore, proclaims the inordinate but justified civic pride of the Florentines. The very heart of the city's *centro storico* (historical centre), it was begun in 1296 under Arnolfo di Cambio, although the imposing green, white and rose marble neo-Gothic façade was completed six centuries later. The first of its glories is the free-standing **campanile** (open daily Apr–Sept 8.30am–7.30pm; Oct 9am–5.30pm; Nov–Mar 9am–4.30pm), designed by Giotto. The 85m (267-ft) bell-tower (it's a 414-stair climb to the top) is decorated on its lower

Brunelleschi's Duomo

sections by hexagonal bas-reliefs sculpted by Andrea Pisano and Luca della Robbia, based on Giotto's drawings. Characteristic of the city's civic consciousness, they portray the Life of Man from Adam's creation to the rise of civilisation through the arts and sciences – music, architecture, metallurgy – pursued so earnestly by the various Florentine guilds that commissioned the work.

Originals of Donatello's sculpture are on display in the cathedral's own museum, the **Museo dell'Opera del Duomo** (Piazza del Duomo; open Mon–Sat 9am–7.30pm, Sun 9am–1.40pm), as well as

The Campanile

Michelangelo's unfinished *Pietà*. The dead Jesus in his mother's arms emphasises the agony rather than the pathos portrayed by the *Pietà* in St Peter's in Rome. Michelangelo conceived the group for his tomb and represented himself in the figure of Nicodemus. Flaws in the marble so enraged the artist that he hurled a hammer at it, destroying Christ's left leg – the left arm has been restored, and the rather insipid Mary Magdalene was later added by a pupil.

Brunelleschi's masterpiece, the cathedral's grandiose terracotta **cupola** (open Mon–Fri 8.30am–7pm, until 5.40pm Sat), with eight white stone ribs curving to the marble lantern at the top, is the city's symbol, visible from far beyond in the Tuscan hills. Completed in 1436, it measures 45.5m (149ft) in diameter. The 463 steps to its top climb in comfortable stages to reveal a panorama of the city, different views of the cathedral's interior

Baptistry of San Giovanni

and close-ups of the dome's 16th-century frescoes restored in 1996. Begun by Giorgio Vasari and finished by his pupil Federico Zuccari, it is the world's largest depiction of the Last Supper. (Brunelleschi's original wooden model of the cupola is displayed in the cathedral museum.) Look for Ghiberti's **bronze shrine** below the high altar, as well as his three stained-glass windows on the entrance wall. In the third bay on the north aisle is Paolo Uccello's statue-like equestrian painting of the 15th-century English mercenary Sir John Hawkwood (unpronounceable for Italians, he is known as *Giovanni Acuto*).

The octagonal 12th-century Romanesque **baptistry** (open Mon–Sat noon–7pm, Sun 8.30am–2pm) of San Giovanni (St John) is celebrated as the oldest building in Florence and for the magnificent bas-reliefs of its three sets of **bronze doors**. The oldest, facing south and telling the story of John the Baptist, was designed by Andrea Pisano in 1330. A century later, Lorenzo Ghiberti won the competition to design the great north and east doors, devoted respectively to the Life of Jesus and to various scenes from the Old Testament. Michelangelo remarked that the latter, which are facing the Duomo, were good enough to adorn the entrance to heaven, and they have been known ever since as the *Doors of Paradise*. Among the losing candidates was Filippo Brunelleschi, who from then on devoted himself entirely to architecture.

The magnificent Byzantine-style **mosaics** inside the cupola include scenes from *The Creation*, *Life of St John* and a *Last Judgment*, and date from the 13th century.

The Medici Palace

The might of the Medici family can be sensed in their massive *palazzo*, northwest of the cathedral on Via Cavour, the 15th-century **Palazzo Medici-Riccardi** (open Thur–Tues 9am–7pm; closed Wed). Now Florence's prefecture offices, the formidable edifice set the style for the city's Renaissance palaces. The ground floor had an open loggia at the corner for the family banking business. The upstairs chapel contains Benozzo Gozzoli's 15th-century **fresco**, *Journey of the Magi to Bethlehem*. It portrays the Medici clan led by Lorenzo the Magnificent in an allegory of an ecumenical council with Pope Pius II in Florence. The Medici family lived here until moving to the Palazzo Vecchio, then the Palazzo Pitti.

Around the corner is the family church of **San Lorenzo** (open Mon–Sat 10am–5pm), designed by Brunelleschi before he worked on the Duomo's cupola. Inside, you'll see the Medici

War and Flood

In the 20th century, the Arno river meant nothing but trouble. To slow the Allied advance in August, 1944, the Germans blew up all of Florence's bridges except the Ponte Vecchio. And in case their enemy planned to drive vehicles across this ancient footbridge, they blocked approaches by destroying buildings within a radius of 200m (219 yards). On 4 November 1966, the river burst its banks and flooded the city, destroying and damaging over 1,000 paintings and 500 sculptures as well as countless precious books and manuscripts in Florence's libraries. In Bargello's Michelangelo Hall you can see wall marks recording the flood level at 3m (10ft) and higher. But in that golden Age of Aquarius, the 1960s' art-loving brothers and sisters poured into the city from all over the world to help with the rescue operation, spearheaded by Florence's own proud citizens.

family arms set in the floor in front of the altar. Brunelleschi is at his most elegant in the **Old Sacristy** at the end of the left transept (site of a few Medici tombs), decorated with four Donatello wall-medallions (the artist is buried in the left transept). Adjacent to the church is the Laurentian Library (*Biblioteca* commissioned in 1524 and known for the graceful cloisters and monumental Michelangelo-designed stairway.

Adjoining the church but with a separate entrance in the back are the **Medici Chapels** (*Cappelle Medicee*; open Tues–Sun 8.15am–4.50pm, closed alternate Sun, holidays 8.30am–1.50pm), monuments to the family dynasty. The **Princes' Chapel** (*Cappella dei Principi*) is a piece of 17th-century baroque bombast in multi-coloured marbles, for which the altar was only completed in 1939. The summit of Medici power is found in Michelangelo's superb **New Sacristy** (*Sagrestia Nuova*), worked on from 1521–34. Lorenzo the Magnificent and his brother Giuliano lie in simple tombs beneath the sculptor's *Madonna and Child*, flanked by less-er artists' statues of the family patron saints Cosmas and Dami-an. Michelangelo's greatest work here is for Lorenzo's grandson, Lorenzo the Duke of Urbino, portrayed as a pensive Roman soldier and his son, Giuliano the Duke of Nemours.

The church of San Lorenzo is next to hundreds of stalls that make up the open-air **Mercato San Lorenzo**, one of Italy's largest tourist markets offering bargains and interesting buys.

Fra Angelico Museum

It's an easy walk to Piazza San Marco and the Dominican **Monastery of San Marco Museum** (open Mon–Fri 8.15am–1.50pm, Sat 8.15am–6.50pm and alternate Sun 8.15am–7pm), an evocative setting for a museum largely devoted to the paint-ings of Florentine-born Fra Angelico (1387–1455), who lived here as a monk. Off the cloister, with its ancient cedar tree, is the Pilgrims' Hospice (*Ospizio dei Pelligrini*) where some of his finest works are found, notably a *Descent from the Cross*. In the monks' cells upstairs, the frescoes of Beato (Blessed) Angelico were intended to be inspirational rather than decorative. His celebrated *Annunciation* faces the top of the stairs, while other outstanding works include the mystic *Transfiguration* in cell six and *Jesus Mocked* in cell seven. In the small refectory is the important Ghirlandaio mural of the *Last Supper*. The Prior's Quarters in the second dormitory (cells 12, 13 and 14) were the home of fire-and-brimstone preacher Girolamo Savonarola from 1481 until his death in 1498. You can see some of his belongings, his portrait by fellow-monk Fra Bartolomeo and the famous picture of his burning at the stake in Piazza della Signoria.

As a museum conceived primarily for students of Florentine painting from the 13th to 16th century, the **Accademia Gallery** ◄ (*Galleria dell'Accademia*; open Tues–Sun 8.15am–6.50pm) at Via Ricasoli, 60, ranks high on Florence's must-see list. Its major interest is in the seven statues by Michelangelo. Six are unfinished – four *Prisoners* (also known as *The Slaves*), *St Matthew* and a *Pietà* – each a fascinating revelation of how Michelangelo released their power from the marble. The Accademia's highlight

Mercato San Lorenzo

Michelangelo's *David*

is the original *David,* which once stood in the Piazza della Signoria (now substituted by a life-size copy). It was carved from a discarded defective column of marble by the artist when he was just 26. Five centuries of wear and tear had taken their toll on the statue, but restoration work, completed in 2004, has returned *David* to its former glory. However, since the restoration, the antiquated air-conditioning system has done an effective job of directing the dirt brought in by visitors to the gallery back on to the statue. Work is now afoot on developing a 'clean-air cage' for David that should be operational by 2006.

In the Piazza Santissima Annunziata, Brunelleschi produced a a pioneering example of the *piazza* as stage-set. In the 1440s he designed the gracefully arched loggia and the **Spedale degli Innocenti** (open Thur–Tues 8.30am–2pm; closed Wed), the first hospital for foundlings in Europe; swaddled babes are the subject of Andrea della Robbia's roundels above the arches. Michelozzo's later Santissima Annunziata church, together with the 17th-century fountains and equestrian statue of Grand Duke Ferdinando, preserve the harmonies of the master's overall design.

Head out of the piazza just north of the hospital towards the Via della Colonna and the **Museo Archeologico** (open Mon 2–7pm, Tues and Thur 8.30am–7pm, Wed, Fri–Sun 8.30am– 2pm). Its important collection of ancient Egyptian, Greek, Roman and Etruscan art forms an alternative to Renaissance overload.

Piazza della Signoria to Piazza Santa Croce

Flanked by some of the city's most stylish boutiques, this quarter's main street retains the commercial tradition of its medieval name, **Via de' Calzaiuoli** (Stocking- and Shoe-makers Street). It connects the Piazza Duomo with the Piazza della Signoria.

If the **Orsanmichele** (open Mon–Fri 9am–noon, Sat–Sun 9am–1pm) looks more like a grain silo than a church, that's because it has been used as both. Formerly an open loggia, it was rebuilt in the early 14th century as a market and then as a church in 1380 converting its Gothic arches to the present ground-floor windows and adding a granary upstairs. The fortress-like exterior is decorated with 14 niches for saints of the major guilds that commissioned the statues (replicas now stand in their place). Look for Ghiberti's vigorous bronze of the city's patron *St John* (east wall, on the Via de' Calzaiuoli); *St Matthew*, the bankers' tax-collector turned apostle (west); Donatello's *St George*, the armourers' dragon-killer (north, a bronze cast of a marble original in the Bargello); *St Mark*, whose vividly sculpted robes do credit to the linen-drapers he protects (south); and Nanni di Banco's outstanding conspiratorial group of *Four Crowned Martyrs* for the sculptors' own guild of stonemasons and wood-workers (north).

Piazza della Signoria is Florence's civic and social centre. Site of the stoic town hall *(Palazzo Vecchio* or *della Signoria)* since 1299, the square bustles in all seasons, not least because it leads to the richest of Italy's art museums, the Uffizi. At the south end of the square is the 14th-century **Loggia della Signoria** (or **dei Lanzi**), transformed from the city fathers' ceremonial grandstand into a guardroom for Swiss mercenary *Landsknechte*. It shelters Benvenuto Cellini's bronze masterpiece, *Perseus* brandishing the severed head of Medusa. Also in the loggia, the spiralling *Rape of the Sabines* of Giambologna (the Flemish artist Jean de Boulogne) is another piece of dazzling virtuosity, donated by the Medici.

In a *piazza* that is an open-air sculpture gallery, more statuary graces the orator's platform along the Palazzo Vecchio's sober façade. To the left of its entrance is a copy of Donatello's *Marzocco*, Florence's heraldic lion, next to his bronze of *Judith and*

The Palazzo Vecchio

Holofernes, which always made the Medici uneasy with its theme of a tyrant decapitated. Getting little attention is 16th-century Bandinelli's clumsy *Hercules and Cacus*, standing in the shadow of Michelangelo's magnificent *David*; this life-size copy was placed here in 1873. Standing against a hostile world of cruel Philistines, Florentines loved to identify with the beauty and courage of the poetic young giant-killer. A commemorative plaque (near the baroque fountain) embedded in the *piazza* marks the spot where Savonarola was executed .

In contrast to the austere Gothic exterior of the **Palazzo Vecchio** (open Fri–Wed 9am–7pm and Thur 9am–2pm; in summer Mon and Fri till 11pm) by Arnolfo di Cambio (architect of the Duomo), Vasari added ornate stucco and frescoes to the first inner courtyard for a Medici wedding in the 1560s (the *palazzo* was a Medici residence until they moved across the river to the Palazzo Pitti). A copy of Verrocchio's delightful bronze cherub tops the porphyry fountain in the centre. Upstairs, the **Salone dei Cinquecento** was built in 1495 for the short-lived Florentine Republic before serving as Duke Cosimo's throne room and, three centuries later, the chamber of Italy's first national parliament. The décor celebrates Florentine power – Vasari frescoes of victories over Siena and Pisa and Michelangelo's *Victory* statue. The second-floor **Sala dei Gigli** (Hall of the Lilies) is brilliantly decorated in blues and golds with Florentine heraldry and vivid Ghirlandaio frescoes of Roman and early Christian history. It adjoins the **Chancery** *(Cancelleria)* where Niccolò Macchiavelli served as secretary to the Florentine Republic. Any world-weary thoughts inspired by the old cynic's portrait and bust are dispelled by Verrocchio's cherub cuddling a dolphin like a baby doll.

The Uffizi

The **Uffizi Museum** (open Tues–Sun 8.15am–6.50pm, sometimes till 10pm in high summer and during festivals) of Italian and European painting stretches in a long U-shape from the Palazzo Vecchio down to the Arno river and back. Duke Cosimo had Vasari design it in 1560 as a series of government offices *(uffizi)*, a mint for the city's florin and workshops for the Medici's craftsmen. Vasari's greatest architectural work, it is now the home of one of the world's most famous and important art galleries. The Uffizi is set to double in size by 2007, allowing masterpieces from the overflowing storerooms to be displayed. It is said the enlarged gallery will outsize the Louvre, in Paris. The first fruit of the new scheme showcase Caravaggio and the early 17th-century painter Guido Reni, including his arresting *David with the Head of Goliath*.

Stop for an occasional peek out of the window over the Arno and Ponte Vecchio and recharge your batteries at the museum's café above the Loggia dei Lanzi. It has lovely views of the *piazza*. Reorganisation makes it hazardous to specify room numbers, but the paintings are generally exhibited chronologically from the 13th to the 18th century; note, however, that parts of the museum may randomly close. Here are some of the highlights:

Giotto breathes warm humanity into his *Madonna Enthroned* (1310), distinguishing it from the formal pictures of the subject by Cimabue and Duccio in the same room. Giotto's *Madonna* polyptych is also distinctive. Some 30 years later comes the *Annunciation* triptych of Simone Martini, with Mary shying away from the archangel Gabriel.

Paolo Uccello shows a dream-like, almost surrealist obsession with his (unsolved) problems of perspective and

> Queues at the Uffizi are common year-round, but tickets can be reserved in advance – enquire at your hotel or the tourist office. For a small fee you can book a ticket by telephoning Firenze Musei, tel: 055 29 48 83 or book online, at least three days in advance, at: <www.weekendafirenze.com>.

Outside the Uffizi, where there are usually queues

merry-go-round horses in his *Battle of San Romano* (1456). It contrasts with the cool dignity of Piero della Francesca in his *Federigo da Montefeltro* and wife *Battista* (1465), portrayed against their Urbino landscape.

Some of the museum's most visited rooms are to come: in his graceful *Allegory of Spring* (1478) and the exquisite *Birth of Venus*, Botticelli achieves an enchanting mixture of sensuality and purity. His Flemish contemporary Hugo van der Goes is more down-to-earth in the realism of his huge triptych *Adoration of the Shepherds* (1478), which influenced Florentine painters such as Ghirlandaio. In the *Baptism of Christ* (1470) of Verrocchio, you can see the earliest identified work of his most famous pupil, Leonardo da Vinci – the background landscape and the angel on the left, beautiful enough to reduce his companion angel to wide-eyed jealousy. Leonardo's *Annunciation* (1472–1477) of a few years later already shows his characteristic gentle tone and feeling for precise detail and the *Adoration of the Magi*, even as an under-drawing left unfinished by his departure for Milan (1481), reveals his revolutionary power of psychological observation.

Northern European Rooms

The Northern European Rooms include a splendid *Portrait of His Father* (1490) by Albrecht Dürer; *Adam and Eve* (1528) by Lucas Cranach the Elder; *Richard Southwell* by Hans Holbein; and a moving *Mater Dolorosa* by Joos van Cleve. In the mystic *Holy Allegory* (1490) of Giovanni Bellini, we can appreciate the typical Venetian serenity even without understanding its symbols. Titian has a superbly sensual *Venus of Urbino* (1538), less Greek goddess than the prince's mistress she probably was and an equally disturbing *Flora* (1515; more works by Raphael and Titian can be found in the Palazzo Pitti). Some are also upset by the eroticism of Parmigianino in his strange but undeniably graceful *Madonna with the Long Neck* (1534) – just look at those elongated fingers – a masterpiece of the sophisticated and subsequently decadent Mannerism that followed the High Renaissance.

There is an intriguing ambiguity to the half-naked peasant youth posing as a *Bacchus* for Caravaggio (1589), but nothing complicated about the straightforward and robust sexiness of the Rubens *Bacchanale*. And compare Caravaggio's mastery of *chiaroscuro* (the play of light and shadow) in the service of realism in his violent *Abraham and Isaac* (1590) with the more contemplative style of Rembrandt in the famous *Old Rabbi* (1658) and other portraits. The only work by Michelangelo in the Uffizi Gallery is the *Holy Family* or *Doni Tondo* (1504), his only known panel painting. Without Michelangelo's strength, or Leonardo's complexity, the third of Italy's three Renaissance giants, Raphael, brings his own powers of clarity and restraint to the *Madonna of the Goldfinch* (1505) and a *Self-Portrait* made when the artist was 23.

Botticelli's *Birth of Venus*

The Vasari corridor, an aerial walkway along the east side of the Ponte Vecchio and hung with the self-portraits of many great artists is open – in theory (by appointment only). However, it is often used as storage space for the Uffizi overflow.

Santa Croce

Designed in the late 13th century by Arnolfo di Cambio (architect of the Palazzo Vecchio and the Duomo) with a neo-Gothic façade added in 1863, the Franciscan church of **Santa Croce** (east of the Uffizi; open Mon–Sat 9.30am–5.30pm, Sun 1–5.30pm), has an important series of **Giotto frescoes**. The pathos shines through the heavily restored paintings of St Francis in the Bardi Chapel (c.1320s), to the right of the apse and two St Johns in the Peruzzi Chapel next door. In a chapel in the left transept, the wooden *Crucifixion* by Donatello (1425) is in affecting naturalistic contrast to the Renaissance idealism of the time.

The church is also the last resting place of Galileo, Machiavelli, Ghiberti and composer Rossini. **Michelangelo's tomb** (right aisle, second bay) was designed by Vasari, with symbolic statues of Painting, Sculpture and Architecture mourning beneath a bust of the Florentine-born artist who died aged 89. The Florentines had to smuggle his body out of Rome.

At the back of the cloister of Santa Croce's monastery adjoining the church, Brunelleschi's **Pazzi Chapel** *(Cappella dei Pazzi)* is a little gem of Renaissance elegance designed in 1443. Luca della Robbia's subdued glazed ceramic roundels depict the 12 Apostles and Four Evangelists. The most cherished treasure in the **Santa Croce Museum** is Cimabue's 13th-century massive *Crucifixion*, rescued and restored after the 1966 flood. It now hangs on an electric cable to be hoisted upwards out of harm's way should another flood ever happen.

The First Town Hall

The ominous 13th-century fortress-like *palazzo* that houses the **Bargello Museum** (Via del Proconsolo, 4; open Tues–Sat and alternate Sun and Mon, 8.15am–1.50pm) was Florence's first town hall and dreaded prison under the jurisdiction of the Police Chief, or *Bargello*, before becoming the National Museum of Sculpture. The old armoury is now the **Michelangelo Hall** *(Sala Michelangelo)* greeting you with a dour bust of the master by Daniele da Volterra. Among the Cellini bronzes is an imposing bust of his master, *Duke Cosimo*. The **General Council Hall** *(Sala del Consiglio Generale)* is dominated by Donatello including his famous *David*, naked and restless in bronze (1450), and the stone *Marzocco* lion, the town's symbol, from the Palazzo Vecchio. You can also see the two bronze panels submitted for the Baptistry doors competition in 1401. On the second floor is a Verrocchio *David* (*c.*1471), for which his 19-year-old pupil Leonardo da Vinci is believed to have been the model.

From the Mercato Nuovo to Santa Maria Novella

Start out from the centre, the heart of medieval Florence, on the street named after the drapers' guild, the **Via Calimala**. Just south

The Bargello and surroundings bathed in golden light

of the café-ringed Piazza della Repubblica is the covered **Merca-to Nuovo**, a 16th-century loggia where the bronze statue of a wild boar, *il Porcellino*, is every Florentine child's favourite. If you rub it's burnished snout and throw a coin in the fountain, your wish for a return trip to Florence is supposed to come true. The market was once called the Straw Market because of the straw products for which Florence was known. These items (bags, place-mats) are now made in China, as are most tourist souvenirs on sale here. The mementos pale in comparison to the open-air **Mercato San Lorenzo**, north of the Duomo near the church of the same name.

West on the Via Porta Rossa is the 14th-century **Palazzo Da-vanzati**, closed at the time of writing for restoration except for a small photographic exhibition (open Tues–Sun 9am–2pm; closed 2nd and 4th Sunday of the month), showing of some of the contents. Its stern, fortress-like exterior has iron rings at ground level for tethering horses and on upper storeys to hold torches and lanterns for festive occasions.

The church of **Santa Trinità** has a late-16th-century baroque façade with a Gothic interior. Ghirlandaio, master teacher of Leonardo da Vinci, decorated the Sassetti Chapel.

Florence's most elegant shops continue along the **Via de' Tornabuoni**. On the 15th-century **Palazzo Strozzi**, look out for the intricate wrought-iron lanterns; the massive *palazzo*, once a private residence, is used for special exhibitions and the biennial antique fair. West of here is the **Via della Vigna Nuova**, where the overspill of Tornabuoni's most exclusive stores continues.

Fresco detail, Santa Maria Novella

The 13th-century Domini-can church of **Santa Maria Novella**, recognisable by its graceful façade in white, green, and pink marble added ◄

by Leon Battista Alberti in 1470, is the finest of Florence's monastic churches (open Mon–Thur and Sat 9.30am– 5pm; Fri and Sun 1–5pm). Among its artistic treasures is one of the city's greatest paintings, the *Masaccio Trinity* (from around 1427; left aisle, third bay), which is famed for its early handling of perspective and depth. The church also has one of Italy's most delightful fresco cycles,

Santa Maria Novella

by Ghirlandaio, of the lives of the Madonna and St John, which kept the master's entire workshop busy from 1485 to 1490. The Filippo Strozzi Chapel (right of the altar) is decorated with Filippino Lippi's frescoes of saints Philip and John. In the Gondi Chapel (left of the high altar) is the Brunelleschi *Crucifixion* (1410) while Giotto's serene *Crucifixion* (1290) is in the Sacristy (left transept).

Through a separate entrance left of the church, escape the bustle of the *piazza* in the Dominicans' 14th-century **cloister** (*Chiostro Verde*), with Paolo Uccello's frescoes of the *Universal Deluge*. The **Spanish Chapel** (*Cappellone degli Spagnoli*) is covered by 14th-century frescoes by Andrea da Firenze.

North of Santa Maria Novella, spare a glance for the simple, clean-lined architecture of the **Stazione Centrale** (main railway station), built in 1935 during Mussolini's heyday but avoiding the bombastic pomposity of the fascist regime.

Heading back down towards the river, have a drink in the plush neo-Renaissance bar of the five-star Westin Excelsior (at No. 3, Piazza Ognissanti, tel: 055 27151 hotel, 055 2715 2785 restaurant) then cross the square to the church of the **Ognissanti** (All Saints Church; open daily; summer 8.30am–12.30pm and 4.30–5.30pm; winter 9am–12.30pm and 3.30–5.30pm), built in the 13th-century

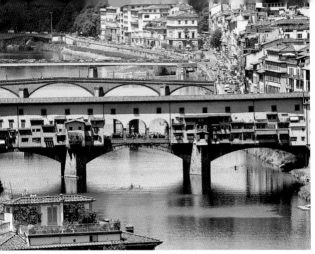

The Ponte Vecchio, Florence's first bridge

with a 1637 baroque façade. Portrayed to the right of Mary in Ghirlandaio's *Madonna of Mercy* (right aisle, 2nd bay) is the Florentine banker-navigator Amerigo Vespucci, who gave his name to the continent of America and whose family was a sponsor of this church. Botticelli is buried in a chapel (right transept). The highlight of the church is Domenico Ghirlandaio's huge fresco of the Last Supper (1480), which is through the cloister in the old refectory, the **Cenacolo** (open Mon, Tues and Sat 9am–noon).

South of the Arno

There's nothing romantic about the murky waters of the Arno river, with broad, 19th-century *lungarni* embankments that protect it from flooding. Of the many bridges that cross it, two are noteworthy. The **Ponte Santa Trinita**, destroyed in 1944, has been rebuilt with the original 16th-century masonry scooped from the bottom of the river, including statues of the *Four Seasons*. Bartolomeo Ammanati's three lovely elliptical arches follow drawings by Michelangelo.

The **Ponte Vecchio**, intact since 1345, was Florence's first and for centuries only, bridge. The boutiques with their back rooms overhanging the river were built from the 16th to the 19th century. Across the tops of these small former workshops, Vasari provided a covered corridor for Duke Cosimo to keep out of the rain when crossing from his Pitti Palace to the Uffizi. The duke didn't like the smell of the bridge's butcher shops and had them replaced by goldsmiths and jewellers, whose descendants offer you their high-quality wares today: this is some of Italy's finest window shopping. A bronze bust (1900) of Italy's celebrated goldsmith, Benvenuto Cellini, holds a position of honour in the middle of the bridge with a vantage point of lovely views.

In Renaissance times, the quarter south of the Arno, Florence's 'Left Bank', was an aristocratic preserve where the Medici held court. Today their sprawling **Pitti Palace** (*Palazzo Pitti*; open Tues–Sun 8.30am–6.50pm; ticket office closes one hour earlier) has four museums and state apartments (following varying and erratic schedules with the exception of the largest and most reliable, the Pitti Gallery). Its dauntingly heavy and graceless façade belies the ornate and colourful interior. Duke Cosimo I and his wife, Eleonora of Toledo, acquired the palace from the bankrupt Pitti merchant family in 1549. As the Medici's official residence, it was enlarged and embellished over the centuries and the rich world of the Medici you can see today is much as they left it.

Statue at the Pitti Palace

The **Pitti Gallery** (*Galleria Palatina*) is the family art collection and the most important in Florence after the Uffizi. The paintings are displayed just as the dukes hung them, up to four-high, by personal preference rather than in historical sequence. The 26 richly-decorated salons (just a fraction of the Medici residence) are named after the themes of their 17th-century frescoes – Venus, Hercules, Prometheus. Family pictures portray princesses, cardinals and popes.

The Medici's taste and means brought a considerable number of masterpieces. Titian displays his masterly use of colour and light in *The Concert* (Hall 5, Venus), a haunting portrait of *The Englishman* and bare-breasted *Magdalen* (Hall 6, Apollo). Rubens shows Venus restraining Mars in his vivid *Consequences of War* and portrays himself on the left of his *Four Philosophers* (Hall 7, Mars). Raphael is well represented by a stately *Veiled Woman* (Hall 8, Jupiter), a classic *Madonna of the Chair* and *Maddalena Doni* (Hall 9, Saturn), deliberately imitating the pose of Leonardo da Vinci's *Mona Lisa* and *Pregnant Women* (Hall 10, Iliad). Caravaggio contributes a typically disturbing canvas, an ugly *Sleeping Cupid* (Hall 32, Education of Jupiter).

Palazzo Pitti

On the next floor is the **Modern Art Gallery** (*Galleria d'Arte Moderna*; open Tues–Sat plus alternate Sun and Mon 8.15am–1.50pm), devoted to 19th- and 20th-century Italian art. Most notable is the work of the *Macchiaioli* school of Tuscan pre-Impressionists, who met at Florence's Caffè Michelangelo in the 1860s seeking freedom from academic art that paralleled the political Risorgimento. Giorgio de Chirico and Eduardo de Pisis are among the more important 20th-century exhibitors.

The Pitti's next-most visited gallery, the **Silverware Museum** (*Museo degli Argenti*), occupies 16 sumptuously decorated rooms to offset the Medici family's treasures – gold, silver, jewels, beautiful 16th- and 17th-century amber and ivory, crystal, porcelain and baroque furniture. The **Costume Museum** (*Museo del Costume*) is a collection of traditional dress from the 18th–20th century. The **Carriage Museum** (*Museo delle Carrozze*), in a wing on the far right of the palace and the **Royal Apartments** (*Appartamenti Monumentali*), upstairs, on the right of the main entrance, show a truly palatial life. (Opening times for all four are as for the Modern Art Gallery, above.)

Boboli Gardens

Take a rest in the shade of the cypresses, pines and holm oaks of the palace's **Boboli Gardens** (open daily June–Aug 8.15am–8pm; Apr, May and Sept 8.15am–7pm; Mar and Oct 8.15am–6pm; Nov–Feb 8.15am–one hour before sunset), which form a Renaissance and baroque theme park dotted with loggias, cool fountains, grottoes with artificial stalactites and myriad statues of gods, nymphs and grotesques (derived from the word 'grotto').

Directly behind the palace, the **Amphitheatre**, shaped like a Roman circus and with lovely views of the Palazzo Pitti and the city beyond, was the scene of the Medici's most extravagant fêtes and staged performances. In the middle of the nearby Pond of Neptune (*Vasca del Nettuno*), the burly sea god wields his trident in petrified parody of one of the Boboli's gardeners.

After the Pitti's overwhelming riches, the unadorned white façade of the nearby Augustinian church of **Santo Spirito** (in

For a last panoramic sunset view of the city, take a bus or taxi to the vast Piazzale Michelangelo (anchored by a second copy of his David). The lovely 11th-century church of San Miniato (up the hill behind the square) is Florence's oldest and one of its most beloved churches. Be there in late afternoon when a handful of resident monks chant timeless Gregorian vespers.

the Piazza Santo Spirito) is a sobering antidote. Brunelleschi's design was never completed but the interior of the church preserves the spatial clarity of his Corinthian-capitaled colonnades. In the right transept is a strikingly theatrical *Madonna Enthroned* by Filippino Lippi.

The church of **Santa Maria del Carmine** (*Copella Brancacci* chapel; open Wed–Mon 10am–5pm, Sun and holidays 1–5pm) is an essential stop on any artistic pilgrimage to Florence. The church itself is an unprepossessing reconstruction after a devastating fire of 1771, but the Brancacci Chapel containing the great **Masaccio frescoes** miraculously survived intact. The bright light of the early years of the Renaissance, the talented painter died at the age of 27 after only five years of promising creative activity (from 1423 to 1428), working with his mild-mannered teacher Masolino on scenes from Genesis and the life of St Peter. Compare Masolino's sweet and harmonious Adam and Eve in his *Original Sin* (chapel entrance, upper right) with Masaccio's agonising figures in the *Expulsion from the Garden of Eden*, opposite, to appreciate one of the early Renaissance's most dramatic statements. Nothing like them had ever been painted before. Florence's greatest artists, Michelangelo at their head, came to gaze and marvel, sketching Masaccio's trail-blazing use of light and visual depth as instruments of emotional impact, particularly striking in the broad sweep of his *St Peter Paying the Tribute Money*. The chapel frescoes were completed in the 1480s by Filippino Lippi, who painted the side walls' lower panels.

Around Tuscany *(Toscana)*

The original territory of the ancient civilisation of the Etruscans has always been independent-minded, even aloof, in its attitude to Rome and the other regions. For the serious Italophile, its beauty and riches deserve weeks, months, even years of attention, but no first visit would be complete without at least a brief foray here. After an easy side-trip from Florence to Fiesole, our itineraries go further afield – west to Pisa and Lucca before turning south through the hills of Chianti to Siena.

Fiesole

Just 8 km (5 miles) northeast of Florence the road winds up a wooded cypress-studded hillside, revealing at each bend ever-changing views of Fiesole's gardens and historical villas and the monuments of the great Renaissance city below. Drivers can negotiate the winding old side-road **Via Vecchia Fiesolana** for glimpses of villas half-hidden among the cypresses and olive trees.

Florence from Fiesole

The town centre, Piazza Mino da Fiesole, with its austere cathedral founded in 1028, is the starting-point for some exhilarating hill walks (the tourist office in Piazza Nino da Fiesole has walking maps), the most immediate being the steep paved lane leading from the square up to the small **San Francesco** convent.

Only some wall fragments remain of the former Etruscan stronghold in Fiesole itself, but there are extensive Roman ruins, including a well-preserved **amphitheatre**, seating 3,000 and dating to the 1st century BC – still in use for summer festivals. Nearby, the **Zona Archeologico** combines the Museo Archeologico, Museo Bandini and Antiquarium Costantani (open daily 9.30am–7pm, closed Tues in winter).

Pisa

In its heyday from the 11th to the 13th century, **Pisa** created a powerful maritime empire down the Tyrrhenian coast and in Corsica, Sardinia, Sicily, Syria, Palestine and Egypt. Its riches and prestige called for a legacy, providing the funds for the gleaming white marble complex of religious edifices known as the **Campo dei Miracoli** (Field of Miracles), of which its leaning bell tower is a national icon. Most rushed visitors see the square, stand in awe of the tilting tower and leave town.

Conquering a flat landscape with serene, other-worldly harmony, this assembly of buildings in an emerald green square also known as the **Piazza del Duomo** celebrates the whole cycle of life, from baptistry, cathedral and campanile (also known as The Leaning Tower) to the monumental cemetery of the Campo Santo. The **Duomo** (open daily Mar 9am–6pm, Apr–Sept 8am–8pm, Oct–Feb 9am–5pm) was begun in 1063 during the Golden Age, to honour Pisa's victory over the Saracens in Sicily. With Oriental and Byzantine decorative elements reflecting the Pisan Republic's overseas interests, its four-tiered arcaded façade over three porches is a masterpiece of grace and delicacy. Architect Buscheto didn't hesitate to write in Latin (in the far left arch) 'This marble church has no equal.' Inside, there was no reason either for local Giovanni Pisano to show false modesty about his superbly sculpted 14th-century **marble pulpit** (left aisle), the cathedral's masterpiece.

Thanks to its unstable subsoil, the **Leaning Tower** *(Campanile*; open daily Apr–Sept 8am–8pm; Mar, Oct 9am–6pm; all other months 9am–5pm; entrance fee; advanced reservation only, tel: 050 560547; <www.duomo.pisa.it>) has always tilted. Begun after the Duomo in 1173, it started to lean when only three of its eight storeys had been completed. The overhang increased over time and by the late 20th century it was 4.5m (15ft) out of alignment. Fearing an imminent collapse, the authorities closed the tower in 1990, while engineers sought a remedy. It was finally decided that soil should be extracted from the foundations on the opposite side to the lean and by early 2001 the top of the tower had been brought back 45cm – a 10 percent reduction in inclination. The tower has reopened to the public, with up to 30 people at a time allowed up the 294 steps of the narrow spiral staircase (tours every 40 minutes).

The Leaning Tower

The lovely circular **Baptistry** *(Battistero*; open summer daily 8am–7.40pm; winter daily 9am–4.40pm), is topped by a traditional statue of John the Baptist. Left of the baptismal font and altar is Pisa's greatest work of sculpture, a hexagonal **marble pulpit** by Nicola Pisano, father of the Giovanni who designed the cathedral pulpit.

Note, in the 13th-century cloistered cemetery of the **Camposanto** (Holy Ground, believed to be filled with sacred dirt brought from the Holy Land during the Crusades – opening hours as for the Baptistry), the Gothic tabernacle enclosing a *Madonna and Saints*. The north gallery of the cloister has a **fresco** of the *Triumph of Death* (1360).

Lucca

The 'sights' of this town take scarcely a day, but the seductive tranquillity within its perfectly preserved ramparts is irresistible. Things were not always so peaceful here. In the stormy 15th and 16th centuries, Lucca's prosperous silk merchants preserved the peace by intercepting enemy armies and paying them to bypass the town. It has been particularly rich in musicians, notably Boccherini and Puccini and hosts a series of music festivals in summer.

Begin with a stroll or bicycle ride on the tree-shaded pathway atop the brick 16th–17th century **ramparts**, along the Passeggiata delle Mura, for a good overall view of the town's traffic-free *centro storico* contained within the walls. Begun in 1060, the **Duomo d' San Martino** (open daily 7am–7pm, till 5pm in winter) has a Pisan-style three-storeyed façade with a *Descent from the Cross* carved by Nicola Pisano over the north door. Its prized possessions are two: the haunting **Volto Santo** (Holy Face), a wooden crucifix said to have been carved by Nicodemus and possessing miraculous

Duomo sculpture, Lucca

powers; and the graceful white marble **tomb of Ilaria del Carretto Guinigi** (open April–Oct Mon–Fri 9.30am– 5.45pm, Sat till 6.45pm, Sun 9am–5.45pm; Nov–March Mon– Fri 9.30am–4.45pm, Sat 9.30–6.45pm, Sun 11.30am– 4.45pm) by master Sienese sculptor Jacopo della Quercia (1408) in the former sacristy.

Northwest of the cathedral is the town's other beloved church, **San Michele in Foro** (open daily 8am–noon and 3–6pm), on the site of the Roman Forum. Begun in 1143, its arcaded façade varies the patterns of its four tiers of columns in pink, green, black, or white marble. With a pair of binoculars, you should be able to spot, on the third tier of arches (third from the right), busts of Risorgimento heroes Garibaldi and Cavour.

Chianti Classico grapes

To capture something of the town's medieval character, explore the **Via Guinigi**, with smart 14th-century palaces, and the towered houses of **Via Fillungo**, leading to the Roman amphitheatre, now the Piazza del Mercato. Nearby, the façade of the church of **San Frediano** has a 13th-century mosaic of the *Ascension of Christ*. In the interior (fourth chapel on left aisle), look for Jacopo della Quercia's marble altar (1422).

Chianti

The best introduction to the Tuscan hill country is a tour of the famous **vineyards** that grace its southern-oriented slopes. The grapes that qualify as *Chianti Classico*, distinguished by a coveted black rooster label, grow in the region between Florence and Siena, most of them along the ancient Via Chiantigiana, which is route S222. The liveliest, most colourful time is during the autumn grape harvest, *la vendemmia*, but tasting – and buying – goes on at many of the Chianti vineyards all year round.

Start out at San Casciano in Val di Pesa, 17 km (11 miles) south of Florence, with a bonus for art-lovers of a Simone Martini *Crucifixion* and other Sienese works in the church of La Misericordia. Southeast across to route S222, you find the characteristic landscape of vineyards interspersed with equally renowned olive groves as you approach Greve, a characteristic town that is the major wine centre for the area. The wine route continues through **Castellina** with its 15th-century castle and ancient town gate. Then on to **Radda**, where you should peep in at the **Piccolo Museo del Chianti** and to **Gaiole in Chianti**, one of the best centres for tasting and a place to linger.

San Gimignano

The haunting silhouette and well-preserved centre make **San Gimignano** the most magical of Tuscany's hill towns. There were once more than 70 towers – erected as symbols of mercantile power and prestige – until the town's Florentine conquerors ordered them to be dismantled in the 14th century. Only 13 remain.

The most important are clustered around three adjoining **squares**: the triangular Piazza della Cisterna named after the city's 13th-century travertine well, surrounded by elegant palaces; the Piazza del Duomo, grouping church and town hall as the seat of civic and religious power; and the Piazza delle Erbe marketplace with twin Salvucci towers.

The 13th-century town hall, **Palazzo del Popolo**, houses the **Museo Civico** and **Pinacoteca** (open daily Mar–Oct 9.30am–7.20pm; Nov–Feb 10am–5.50pm). The latter includes a *Crucifixion* by Coppo di Marcovaldo and a Taddeo di Bartolo painting of St Gimignano, in which you can see what the towers of the medieval city looked like. The Palazzo's Torre Grossa, the only climbable tower in San Gimignano, offers great views.

The 12th-century Romanesque **Collegiata** (open Mar–Oct Mon–Fri 9.30am–7.30pm, Sat 9.30am–5pm, Sun 1–5pm; Nov–mid-Jan Mon–Sat 9.30am–5pm, Sun 1–5pm; closed late Jan–Feb) is known as the town's *duomo*, despite the fact that it is not officially a cathedral. Along the right aisle are dramatic frescoes of New Testament scenes. The Ghirlandaio **frescoes** in the Santa

> **The most photogenic view of San Gimignano is from the north, on the road from Certaldo, home and the last resting place of Boccaccio, author of *The Decameron*.**

San Gimignano's 'Manhattan' skyline

Fina Chapel (at the end of the right aisle) are a series of sophisticated social portraits (1475) dedicated to the young patron saint of San Gimignano. By the east wall, flanking the church entrance, are wooden statues of Mary and the Archangel Gabriel by Jacopo della Quercia.

To view Tuscany at its most poetic, climb up to the ruins of the **Rocca** citadel, the town's highest point and a good picnic spot.

Volterra

This fortified town perched high on its hill works a sober charm among the buff-stone 13th-century edifices of its **Piazza dei Priori** and adjacent Piazza San Giovanni. The Palazzo dei Priori (1208) is the oldest of Tuscany's typical town halls, with a two-tiered tower, battlements and mullioned windows. It stands opposite the massive triple-arched **Palazzo Pretorio**, medieval police headquarters. The two squares are separated by the 12th-century cathedral and 13th-century octagonal baptistry. The latter's baptismal font has bas-reliefs by Andrea Sansovino.

Away from the centre, you can trace the town's beginnings in the **Museo Etrusco Guaranacci** (Via Don Minzoni, 15; open daily summer 9am–7pm; Nov–mid-Mar 9am –2pm). The collection includes sculpted stone, alabaster and terracotta funeral urns dating back to the 6th century BC. Volterra is known for its alabaster production as a glimpse in any shop window will confirm.

Siena

A time-locked city of rich russet browns and weathered ochres, **Siena** is as perfectly medieval as greystone Florence is a Renaissance showcase, yet contrasts with its centuries-old rival to the north are striking and inevitable. Whereas the nucleus of Florence was built to a strict Roman city plan of straight streets intersecting at right angles, Siena has all the Tuscan hill-town's haphazard organic forms, straggling up and down a forked ridge of three hilltops. Closed to traffic (and free of taxis), it is not for the weak of knee.

Siena, a perfectly medieval city

While Florentine art developed its formidable intellectual and emotional power, the tone of Sienese painting – Simone Martini, the Lorenzettis, even the Mannerist Sodoma – remained gentle and delicate, bathed in the light and colour of its surrounding countryside. But as its obstinately independent spirit has shown, even after the Florentine conquest of 1555 – a spirit epitomised by its lusty Palio tournament – the town is not without vigour. Like an open-air museum, Siena is still a very dignified lived-in town, with fashionable restaurants and boutiques, a vibrant local pride nurtured by economic stability and a rich historic legacy.

At its heart is the sloping, fan-shaped **Piazza del Campo**, site of the old Roman forum and arena of the town's world-famous annual Palio horse race *(see next page)*. The unique *piazza*'s red-brick herringbone paving is divided by nine marble strips for the nine patrician clans that ruled the city at the end of the 13th century.

The painterly impact of the 'burnt sienna' glows from the arcaded Gothic **Palazzo Pubblico**, with its grand 102-m (335-ft) **Torre del Mangia** (open daily 10am–7pm, till 4pm Nov– Feb) – climb to its first tier at 88m (288ft) for a magnificent view of the city and countryside beyond. The loggia at the tower's base is a chapel *(Cappella di Piazza)* marking the city's deliverance from the plague of 1348. Note that there are 503 steps in total.

The Palazzo Pubblico's ground floor houses the offices of the town hall, but its upstairs chambers, frescoed by the city's foremost artists, have been transformed into a **Museo Civico** (municipal museum; open daily 10am–7pm; Nov–mid-Mar 10am–5.30pm). The **Sala del Mappamondo** (named after a lost map of the Sienese world painted by Ambrogio Lorenzetti to trace the city's international banking interests) has two great frescoes by the Siena-born master Simone Martini. To the left is the stately *Maestà* (Madonna Enthroned; 1315) and to the right, *Guidoriccio da Fogliano* (1328, but whose authenticity has been disputed), depicting the Sienese captain's ride to a historic victory at Montemassi – in the nicely detailed Tuscan landscape, notice the little Chianti vineyard in the military encampment. In the **Sala della Pace** (Hall of Peace, council chamber of the Nine Patricians), the full force of Siena's civic pride strikes home in the impressive allegorical frescoes (1337–39) by another local master, Ambrogio Lorenzetti. One wall is devoted to *Bad Government*, a gloomy portrait of Tyranny; the other two to Siena's own enlightened *Good Government*, full of fascinating detail of town life – roof-builders, shoe shop, school, outdoor tavern, ladies dancing in the street – and hunters riding out to the surrounding countryside. A second-floor loggia is adorned with Jacopo della Quercia's 15th-century carvings for the city fountain Fonte Gaia.

Southwest of the Campo, the **Duomo** (open Mar–mid-Oct Mon–Sat 7.30am–7.30pm, Sun 2–7.30pm; mid-Oct–Feb Mon–Sat 7.30am–5pm, Sun 2–5pm), built from the 12th to the 14th century, is for many the greatest of Italy's, possibly all of Europe's, Gothic cathedrals. For some, it is a tasteless iced cake – John Ruskin, for example, dismissed it as 'over-striped…a piece of costly confectionery and faithless vanity'. The interior continues the bands of black-and-white marble that decorate the exterior, while elaborately **inlaid marble paving** – one of the cathedral's primary attractions, with large sections regularly covered for protection – covers the floor with 56 pictures of biblical and allegorical themes, done over two centuries by some 40 artists. The early-16th-century **Cardinal Piccolomini Library** (open mid-

---

Riding for the Palio

The Palio horse race, held on 2 July (7.45pm) and 16 August (7pm), is part of a traditional pageant dating to before the 15th century. Colourful Renaissance-costumed pages and men-at-arms put on a procession and show of flag-throwing with emblems – eagle, snail, porcupine, goose and others – of the 17 parishes *(contrade)* of the city and surrounding communes. Ten of them compete in the climactic breakneck bareback horse race round the Campo for which a painted silk standard, the Palio, is the prize. The race lasts about a minute and a half. To avoid the crush of spectators in the square, reserve a seat in a stand or a place on a balcony well in advance. Contact Palio Viaggi, tel: 05 7728 0828.

Mar–Oct Mon–Sat 9am–7.30pm, Sun 2–5pm; Nov–mid-Mar Mon–Sat 10am–1pm, Sun 2–5pm), off the left aisle, is vividly decorated by Pinturicchio's action-packed frescoes of the life of Pope Pius II (the locally born Piccolomini cardinal himself became pope, Pius III, but lasted only 10 days). In the left transept is a magnificent octagonal 13th-century pulpit carved by Nicola Pisano in which the damned are being eaten alive in the *Last Judgment*. The 17th-century baroque Madonna del Voto Chapel (in the right transept) was designed by Bernini. His statues of St Jerome and Mary Magdalen flank the entrance.

The Duomo's inlaid marble floor

In the **Cathedral Museum** (*Museo dell'Opera Metropolitana*; open daily mid-Mar–Sept 9am–7.30pm; Nov–mid-Mar 9am–1.30pm; Oct 9am–6pm) the focal point is the *Enthroned Madonna* (1308) by local wonder boy Duccio di Buoninsegna. Simone Martini's *Miracles of St Agostino Novello* and Pietro Lorenzetti's *Birth of Mary* are not to be missed.

The importance of Siena's 13th- and 14th-century school of art is illustrated in the imposing Palazzo Buonsignori's **National Art Gallery** (*Pinacoteca Nazionale*; open Tues–Sat 8.15am–7.15pm, Mon, Sun 8.30am–1.30pm). Besides the works of the 14th-century masters Duccio, Pietro and Ambrogio Lorenzetti, as well as Simone Martini, see Siena's 16th-century Mannerists: Beccafumi's dreamy *Birth of Mary* and a highly decorative *Christ at the Column* by Sodoma.

Montepulciano, famous for its wine

Montepulciano and Monte Argentario

South of Siena is a little-trammelled niche of Tuscany and some of the region's most attractive hill towns with excellent local wines. **Montepulciano** (famous for its superb Vino Nobile di Montepulciano), perched 610m (2,000ft) above sea level, is known as 'The Pearl of the 16th Century'. A stroll along the Via di Gracciano and Via Ricci to see the town's noble Renaissance *palazzi* will explain why.

The **Piazza Grande**, the highest point in town, is the site of the graceful town well decorated with griffins and lions. The 13th-century Gothic **Palazzo Comunale** (Town Hall) is a particularly imposing expression of civic dignity. In the austere 16th–17th century **cathedral**, see Taddeo di Bartolo's fine triptych on the high altar. Antonio da Sangallo the Elder, architect of many of the town's *palazzi*, built his masterpiece, the 16th-century church of **San Biagio**, southwest of town, a gem of High Renaissance architecture hidden at the end of a cypress-lined road with views of the Chiana valley. The nearby towns of

Montalcino (known for its Brunello wines) and **Pienza** (the first example of Renaissance urban planning) promise small-town distractions and culinary pleasures.

If you're taking the coast road to or from Rome during warm-weather months, stop off at the fashionable seaside resorts on the pine-forested peninsula of Montepulciano beside the town of **Orbetello**. The sandy beaches and yachting harbours of **Port' Ercole** and **Porto Santo Stefano** are favourite weekend destinations for well-heeled Romans, but they're much quieter during the week. Take a boat excursion out to the pretty island of **Giglio**, one of the islands of the Tuscan archipelago that includes Elba, best known as the island of Napoleon's retreat.

Umbria

Umbria has a less glamorous reputation than Tuscany, but it's highly appreciated both for its great artistic treasures and the dreamy rolling green landscapes that inspired them. The area was dominated in the past by the papacy, which conquered the Lombard dukes of Spoleto in the Middle Ages, Perugia in the 16th century and held sway until the unification of Italy. Apart from pilgrims streaming to St Francis's Assisi and university students heading for Perugia, it has remained – at least in the eyes of foreign visitors – a very happy backwater.

Orvieto

Half the pleasure of this lovely town dramatically perched on a rocky precipice is a first glimpse from afar. For a good view, approach it from the southwest, on route S71 from Lake Bolsena, or look across from the medieval abbey La Badia (now a hotel, tel: 076 330 1959), 8 km (5 miles) south of town.

Connoisseurs come for its white wine, but it's the **cathedral** ◄ (open daily Apr–Sept 7.30am–12.45pm, 2.30pm–7.15pm; Mar and Oct 2.30pm–6.15pm; Nov–Feb 2.30pm–5.15pm), a magnificent Gothic building, that attracts art-lovers. More than 100 architects worked on the church between 1290 and 1600, (its central bronze doors were added in 1964). The highlight is the gleaming **façade** with four slender spired pilasters and a rose-window above the beautifully scrolled porches. At the base of the two northern pilasters, look closely at Lorenzo Maitani's marvellous carved marble **bas-reliefs** of scenes from the Old Testament and the Last Judgement.

Grey and white bands of marble give the interior a spacious simplicity. Off the right transept, the **San Brizio Chapel** (*Cappella Nuova*; open daily 10am–12.45pm and 2.30–7.15pm Apr–June, closes 5.45pm Sun; Mar–Oct 10am–12.45pm and 2.30–6.15pm, Sun 2.30–5.45pm; Nov–Feb Mon–Sat 10am–noon and 2.30–5.15pm, Sun 2.30–5.45pm) is famous for Fra Angelico's 1447 frescoes *Christ in Glory* covering the ceiling and Luca Signorelli's glorious cycle *The Last Judgement* (*c.* 1500) on the walls. To the left, Signorelli portrays himself and Fra Angelico as bystanders in the vivid *Preaching of the Antichrist* (identified here with Savonarola). On the right, the nude figures in the *Resurrection of the Dead* are less convincing,

Orvieto's magnificent Gothic cathedral

echoing da Vinci's comparison to 'sacks of nuts'.

The **Cathedral Museum** in the Palazzo Soliano includes other works by Signorelli, a Simone Martini polyptych and sculpture by Nino, Andrea and Giovanni Pisano.

To cool off, explore the **Pozzo di San Patrizio** (open daily Apr–Sept 10am–6.45pm; Oct–Mar 10am–5.45pm), a 16th-century well that is dug 63m (206ft) into the volcanic rock on the northeast edge of the precipice. Lit by 72 windows, two spiral staircases of 248 steps go down to water level. The town sits on a labyrinth of tunnels, caves and storerooms carved into the tufa begun by the Etruscans and elaborated by the Romans. Guided visits to these depths explore Orvieto's history.

> On 26 September 1997, two major earthquakes rocked Umbria, leaving 10 dead. International media focused on the damage caused in Assisi, but much of the region suffered structural damage and many frescoes and monuments throughout Umbria were severely damaged or destroyed.

Spoleto

The greatest attractions in hill-town Spoleto, 50 km (30 miles) southeast of Orvieto, are the summer music and arts festivals (in particular the Spoleto Festival in June and July), but the town's beautiful natural setting amid wooded hills also makes it a base for country hikes. Especially popular is the oak forest (and monastery) on Monteluco, favoured by St Francis and St Bernardino of Siena.

An important Roman outpost with an excavated first century amphitheatre as proof, Spoleto also boasts a sober Romanesque **cathedral** (open daily 7.30am–12.30pm and 3–6pm; till 5pm in winter) in the medieval Upper Town. Its 17th-century additions are decorated with damaged but still graceful Fra Filippo Lippi frescoes (1469). The tomb for the licentious painter-monk who seduced Sister Lucrezia (the model for many of his Madonnas) was designed by Filippino Lippi, the son of Filippo and Lucrezia.

Assisi

The enduring appeal of St Francis (1182–1226) has turned his native pink-hued town into Italy's major pilgrimage destination, second only to Rome. Its basilica, like the peaceful medieval town centre, has been beautifully preserved and the centuries-old pilgrim trade manages (sometimes just barely) to avoid the unashamed commercialism that blights other religious shrines.

➤   The **Basilica of San Francesco** (open daily Apr–Sept 6.30am–7.30pm; Oct–Mar 7am–5.50pm; note that both churches may close for lunch noon–2pm in winter) is in fact two churches, one above the other, built on top of the saint's simple tomb in the crypt. The epicentre of the 1997 earthquake was located to the east in the Marche. However, several priceless frescoes were severely damaged or destroyed, notably invaluable works by Cimabue (1226–1337) featured on a portion of the Upper Church's vaulted ceiling, which plunged to the floor during the quakes. Following restoration, the basilica reopened in late 1999.

The **Lower Basilica** was begun in 1228, two years after Francis' death and in the year of his canonisation and the frescoes

---

St Francis of Assisi

The spoiled son of a rich family, Francesco di Bernardone was known for his profligate ways. But a sojourn in a Perugia jail at 23, followed by a severe illness, sobered him up. After a vision in the Chapel of San Damiano, he vowed a life of poverty in the service of the Church. He nursed lepers, converted bandits and travelled to Spain, Morocco, Egypt and Palestine. But it was his impact on a troubled Italian population that mattered most to a Church beleaguered by heresy. Thousands responded to the simple eloquence of his preaching. They told how the example of his gentle life had tamed wild wolves and taught swallows to sing more sweetly. In his religious ecstasy on Monte La Verna (near Arezzo), he was marked with Christ's stigmata – a phenomenon the most sceptical scholars have never placed in doubt. He was canonised two years after his death in 1226.

were painted in the 14th century, but a Renaissance porch now precedes the Gothic side entrance. Simone Martini decorated the **St Martin Chapel** (first left) with fine frescoes, including an aristocratic Jesus appearing in St Martin's dream. Stairs in the nave lead to the crypt and St Francis's tomb, rediscovered in 1818, after it had been hidden from plunderers.

Assisi's Eremo delle Carceri

The superb frescoes of the life of Jesus in the **St Mary Magdalen Chapel** and of St Francis's vows of poverty, chastity and obedience above the high altar are attributed to Giotto (1307). In the right transept, Cimabue's **portrait of St Francis** shows him to the right of the Madonna. In the left transept is Pietro Lorenzetti's *Descent from the Cross*. In the **Upper Basilica** Cimabue's works in the apse and left transept have turned black because of the oxidized white lead in his paints, yet you can still feel the intensity of the crowd's anguish in his *Crucifixion*.

In the nave, the faithful are exalted by one of the most grandiose series of **frescoes** in Christendom and, sadly, some of the most damaged in the 1997 earthquake. Generally accepted as the work of a young Giotto, the *Life of St Francis* (1296–1304) is celebrated in 28 scenes along the lower tier (from the right transept), while 32 frescoes in the upper tier illustrate scenes from the Bible.

The Historic Town

Penetrate the historic heart of Assisi along the **Via San Francesco**, with its 15th-century Pilgrims' Hostel (*Oratorio dei Pellegrini*) at No. 11 with frescoes are attributed to Perugino. The noble **Piazza del Comune** forms the town centre, where medieval *palazzi* are grouped around the old Roman forum. The church of **Santa Maria sopra Minerva**, distinguished by its Corinthian columns,

Underground Perugia

was built on the site of a Roman temple under Augustus. A small **Pinacoteca** art museum is across the square.

The 11th-century church of **San Damiano** (open daily 10am–12.30pm and 2–6pm; closes 4.30pm in winter) is a pleasant 1.5-km (1-mile) stroll from the Porta Nuova and is a point of pilgrimage for those interested in the wooden crucifix that spoke to a 27-year-old Francis in 1209 (note that the crucifix is now on show in Assisi's Basilica di St Chiara). Also worth the 4.5-km (2-mile) trip from the town is the **Eremo delle Carceri**, a hermitage founded by St Francis and now a convent.

Perugia

Dominating the Umbrian countryside from its 494-m (1,600-ft) hill, **Perugia** is emphatically more secular and more profane than its mystical Umbrian neighbour Assisi. But the imposing weight of its past is lightened by the lively cosmopolitan student population of its two universities and its contemporary popularity as the sight of one of Europe's most important jazz festivals each July. Perugia's antiquity is symbolised on the north side of town by the **Arco Etrusco** (Etruscan – and partly Roman – triumphal arch) that was incorporated into its medieval ramparts.

In its picture-perfect town centre is the formidable **Palazzo dei Priori** (town hall). Nicola Pisano carved the 13th-century **Fontana Maggiore** (Great Fountain), a favourite rendezvous in the shadow of the 14th-century cathedral. The fourth floor of the town hall (entrance on Corso Vannucci) contains the **Galleria Nazionale dell'Umbria** (open daily 8.30am–7.30pm), a modernised setting for a splendid collection of Umbrian and Tuscan paintings from the 13th–18th century. It includes a Fra Angelico triptych and Piero della Francesca's *Annunciation* and *Madonna with Angels*. But Umbria's pride and joy is the work of Perugia-born Pietro Vanucci, or Perugino (1445–1523). Next door on Corso Vannucci is the **Collegio del Cambio** (open Mar–Oct Mon–Fri and Sun 9am–12.30pm and 2.30–5.30pm, Sat 9am–12.30pm; Nov–Feb Tues–Fri and Sun 9am–2pm, Sat 9am–12.30pm), 15th-century hall and chapel of the bankers' guild where the **Audience Hall** *(Sala dell'Udienza)* is its highlight, covered with Perugino frescoes (1496–1500), seen as his masterpiece.

There is no flagship shop or outlet for the Perugia chocolate industry (which created the Perugino **bacio** or 'chocolate kiss' in 1922), though some of the larger cafés carry some of the confections produced by the local factory, which is open to the public.

Gubbio

Some 40 km (25 miles) north of Perugia, this no-nonsense stalwart hill town is not easy to get to and its steep cobbled streets are hard to navigate. But for anyone who cherishes the tranquillity of an unspoiled medieval atmosphere, Gubbio is a delight.

The brick-paved **Piazza della Signoria** is the centre stage of 'the city of stone'. Its 14th-century crenellated **Palazzo dei Consoli** is one of the grandest civic edifices in Italy and from the *piazza* the *palazzo*'s belltower gives a magnificent panorama. Take one of the lifts hewn into the rocks up to the cathedral and the Renaissance courtyard of the 15th-century Palazzo Ducale. In warm months an open *funivia* (cable-car) brings you up to the basilica of Sant'-Ubaldo, the town's patron saint. Walk from there to the 12th-century fortress of **La Rocca** for unmatched views of the Appennine Mountains.

Unspoiled Gubbio

THE NORTHEAST

Throughout Italy's history, its northeast regions have linked the country to the exotic outside world of Byzantium and the Orient through Venice and its Repubblica Serena and to the Alpine countries north of the Dolomites, while the plains of Emilia-Romagna from Ravenna to Parma provided an anchor to the heartland of the Po valley.

The result is a rich variety of distinctive cities and colourful hinterland. The afterglow of Venice's once-powerful empire is undimmed. Elegant Palladian villas grace the Veneto mainland from Venice to Padua and Vicenza. The glories of Verona extend from its grand Roman arena to the palaces of medieval and Renaissance families whose intrigues and love stories inspired Shakespeare. In Emilia-Romagna, the pride and creativity of the great city-states is still much in evidence in the monuments and museums of Bologna, Ferrara and Parma. Stretch your muscles in the Dolomites with first-class winter sports and summer hiking, or soak up sun and sea in the Adriatic resorts around Rimini.

Venice *(Venezia)*

The incomparable *palazzi*, canals and lagoons of Venice claim a place apart in our collective imagination. In this new millennium, it remains a dreamworld more than ever, its myth more powerful than its harsh reality. Even when it threatens to disintegrate into nightmare at times of winter floods, Carnival shenanigans, or summer hordes, visitors can take refuge in a café once frequented by Casanova or in a back alley and continue their dream uninterrupted. One of the city's many blessings is that there remain so many

> **Visit Venice in May or October if you can – the crowds at Easter and in June to September can be horrible. Venice at Christmas has become fashionable and Carnival commercial. In winter months Venice is dank and cold but has a mystical beauty.**

The Grand Canal and Rialto Bridge, Venice

quiet and beautiful corners, hidden away in the narrow streets, that have changed little with time. Another obvious bonus, impossible to over-emphasise, is the absence of cars, the simple joy of wandering around a town relieved of traffic noise and fumes, of standing on a little humpback pedestrian bridge far from the Grand Canal and hearing only the water lapping against the moss-covered walls, or the occasional swish of a sleek gondola that appears out of nowhere. Staying here forever is most likely to cross your mind.

Try to avoid high summer months, but whatever time of year you go, don't try to see Venice all in a day. Without the time to meander and explore those hidden corners, you risk not seeing much more than Piazza San Marco and understanding little of the city's inherent charm.

Give yourself a minimum of three days, time to get lost (you're never far from the landmarks signposted with bright yellow arrows). The city has more than enough sights to see, but you can taste much of its pleasures before setting foot inside the museums, churches and monuments.

Grand Canal (Canal Grande)

From the railway station or the parking lot of Piazzale Roma, begin with a *vaporetto* waterbus along the **Grand Canal**, the most unique and stunning main 'street' in the world. Use this wonderful first contact with the city as your introductory (and inexpensive) tour. Vaporetto No. 1 takes you to the historic centre of town, Piazza San Marco. Accelerated lines miss out on many of the canal's sites; airport motor launches cross directly to San Marco from the Lido so drop your bags off at the hotel and then hop on the No. 1 in the opposite direction, round-trip. Save your gondola ride – yes, it's touristy and expensive but not to be missed – for when you're settled in.

Along the Grand Canal's 3.8km (more than 2 miles), varying in width from 30 to 70m (100 to 230ft), are the old trading headquarters and warehouses of its distant commercial heyday. Known locally as *ca'* (short for *casa,* or house) as well as *palazzo*, the marble, brick and white-limestone palaces range over 600 years from Venetian-Byzantine to Renaissance, baroque and Neoclassical, but most of them are exotically 14th- and 15th-century Gothic, Venice's 'trademark' in architectural styles. Their sea-resistant limestone foundations stand on massive pinewood stilts driven 8m (26ft) into the lagoon bed.

Going, Going, Gondola

The fleet of 10,000 gondolas of a century ago has dwindled to a few hundred, while the prices have gone in the opposite direction. Apart from commuters taking cross-canal ferry gondolas, Venetians leave the sleek and slender black craft to the tourists. Still handing on the business from father to son, the gondoliers in their straw hats and sailors' jumpers or striped T-shirts are as cheerful and witty as any other taxi-driver. Sadly, they don't sing as often or as well as they used to. Exorbitant yes, but how will you explain to grandchildren, after the last of the gondolas have disappeared, that you visited Venice and never experienced one?

The superb Renaissance **Palazzo Vendramin-Calergi**, where Richard Wagner died in 1883, is today the winter casino. The gilt has gone from the freshly restored façade of the 15th-century Ca' d'Oro *(see page 133)*, but it's still the town's most beautiful and best preserved of the city's Gothic palaces. Italy's most impressive post office, **Fondaco dei Tedeschi** was once the trading-centre of Czechs, Hungarians and Austrians as well as the Germans of its name. Just beyond, the shop-lined white marble **Rialto Bridge** arches the canal at its narrowest point. The 18th-century **Palazzo Grassi** has been restored by Gae Aulenti for major art exhibitions. The prefecture puts its bureaucrats in the fine Renaissance **Palazzo Corner** (or *Ca' Grande)*, while gondoliers claim Othello's Desdemona lived in the lovely late-Gothic **Palazzo Contarini-Fasan**.

The 700-year-old **Fondaco dei Turchi** was a warehouse used by the merchants of Constantinople, now the **Natural History Museum**, which underwent restoration in 2002. It stands next to the plain brick, 15th-century **Megio** wheat granary, decorated by battlements and the republic's seal of St Mark's lion. The imposing 17th-century **Ca' Pesaro** (also restored in 2002) houses the Modern Art Museum *(see page 131)*. Come back early in the morning to look at the covered 20th-century, neo-Gothic **Pescheria** (fish market) and its adjoining produce market. The university has a department in the handsome

Ca' Pesaro

15th-century Gothic **Ca' Foscari**. The **Ca' Rezzonico** is itself a fine specimen of the 18th-century Venetian art for which it is now a museum. Beyond the wooden Accademia Bridge and the **Accademia Art Museum**, the perspective is completed by the magnificent baroque church of **Santa Maria della Salute** that marks the arrival at (or departure from) Piazza San Marco.

Around Piazza San Marco

Building-space on the water being what it is, Venice has only one real *piazza* (all others are called *campi*), but in comparison, any other contender would have died of shame anyway. Gloriously open to sky and sea, **Piazza San Marco** – to locals, just 'the Piazza' – embodies the whole compass of Venetian history and adventure. Its airy arcades reach out to the 900-year-old basilica and turn a corner past the soaring brick campanile to the piazzetta and landing stage of St Mark's basin *(il Bacino)*, historic gateway to the Adriatic and distant ports beyond. For centuries, the odysseys of victorious commanders and commercial ventures of local merchants began and ended here.

This is where the thousand-year-old Repubblica Serena fell in 1797 to Napoleon. While he was busy removing the four ancient bronze horses from the basilica's façade (since returned) along with other art treasures to ship back to Paris, he was said to remark that the Piazza San Marco was 'the world's most beautiful salon'. He closed off the piazza's west end with an Ala Napoleonica (Napoleonic Wing), through which you now enter the **Museo Correr**, devoted to paintings and documents of Venetian history.

Carnival masks

The north and south arms of the square, the 16th-century **Procuratie Vecchie** and

Piazza San Marco, the heart of Venice

Procuratie Nuove, were the residences of the republic's most senior officials. They are now lined with Murano glass and souvenir boutiques, exclusive jewellery and lace shops and, most important for weary or hungry travellers, elegant 18th-century cafés. During the Imperial Austrian rule, the enemy frequented **Quadri** on the north side, while Italian patriots met only at **Florian**, opposite. In warm weather months, their spirited four-piece orchestras play everything from *Moon River* to classical music and Neapolitan love songs. To catch the basilica and square bathed in moonlight is a magical experience.

The glittering façade of the **Basilica di San Marco** (open Mon–Sat 9.30am–5pm, Sun 2–5pm, till 4pm in winter, but daily from 7am for worshippers) forms an exotic backdrop, illuminating Venice's unique role at the crossroads of Eastern and Western culture. What began in AD830 as the Doges' chapel for the remains of the evangelist Mark, the republic's patron saint, was rebuilt in the 11th century as a grandiose Byzantine-Oriental basilica influenced by the Hagia Sofia in Constantinople. Greek mosaicists were brought in to decorate the arches and domes. Five

The famous bronze horses

Romanesque portals correspond to the five Islamic-style domes covering the church's Greek-cross ground plan. With its five mosque-like domes, it is the most sumptuously exotic and Orientally inspired church ever built in the Roman Catholic world.

The first portal on the left is the only one decorated with an original 13th-century mosaic, depicting the *Transfer of St Mark's Body*, smuggled out of Alexandria in Egypt. Mosaics also show the basilica with the famous bronze horses brought from Constantinople after the Crusade of 1204 (the ones over the triple-arched main entrance are copies; since their recent restoration, the originals have been kept in the basilica museum, the Museo Marciano *(see opposite)*.

The Church of Gold

There is a soft glow in the gilded interior from the **mosaics**, illuminated by high stained-glass windows and reflected in the worn patina of the inlaid-marble flooring. Entire books have been written about the original mosaics on the five domes and the great barrel vaults separating them, dating from the 11th–15th century. Among the best are the 12th-century *Pentecost* dome in the nave and the central dome's 13th-century *Ascension*. Others have been heavily restored or replaced, not with true mosaics, but with reproductions in coloured stone of drawings by such artists as Bellini, Mantegna and Tintoretto. The whole is worthy of its nickname, 'church of gold'.

The imposing **high altar** stands over St Mark's tomb. Behind it is the basilica's greatest treasure, the **Pala d'Oro** (Golden Altarpiece), dating back 1,000 years and bejewelled in the 14th century. Guides will tell you that its 255 enamelled panels were encrusted by master Venetian and Byzantine artisans with close to 2,000 precious stones, including pearls, garnets, sapphires, emeralds and rubies. It requires an entrance fee, as does the **Tesoro** (Treasury), a collection of the Crusaders' plunder. To the left of the high altar is a small chapel of the 10th-century *Madonna di Nicopeia*, a bejewelled icon from Constantinople; it is said to have healing powers and is a runner-up as Venice's protective patron after St Mark.

Steep stairs to the right of the main entrance lead to the small **Museo Marciano**, where you can see the original four tethered **bronze horses**, dating from the 2nd or 3rd century AD and a privileged close-up of the basilica's mosaic ceilings from the open galleries. From the outdoor **Loggia dei Cavalli**, you get an excellent view over the Piazza San Marco.

To the right of the loggia (north of the basilica), is the **Torre dell'Orologio** (Clock Tower), under restoration and swathed in scaffolding. Its clock mechanism, all gilt and polychrome enamel, keeps perfect time, activating statues of two green bronze Moors that hammer out the hour. For centuries, the clock tower has been every Venetians favourite rendezvous point, an arched ground-level entranceway leading to the Merceria, a zig-zagging boutique-lined street that cuts through this ancient quarter north to the Rialto Bridge.

The piazza's **Campanile** (belltower; open daily 9am–9pm in high summer; Apr, June, Sept and Oct 9am–7pm; Nov and Mar 9am–4pm), at 99m (324ft), is the highest structure in the city with its belfry, lighthouse, weather vane and gun turret. Emperor Frederick III rode his horse up its spiral ramp (tourists can opt for the lift). Criminals were suspended from it in wooden

Coffee on Piazza San Marco

cages. In 1902, the campanile cracked and collapsed unexpectedly. Ten years later, on its 1,000th anniversary, it was rebuilt using much of the original brick and rescuing one of its five historic bells that is still used today: *'com'era, dov'era'* ('as it was, where it was'). Its collapse crushed Jacopo Sansovino's beautiful 16th-century Loggetta, equally lovingly restored as the entrance to the campanile's lift.

The two tall **columns** facing out over St Mark's Basin were brought from Constantinople in the 12th century. They are topped by statues of St Mark's winged lion and the city's first patron saint, Theodore (replaced by St Mark), with his dragon.

The Doge's Palace

On the waterfront sits the **Doge's Palace** *(Palazzo Ducale)*, for 900 years the focus of Venice's power and pomp, evoked in the imposing elegance of its delicate pink marble and white limestone façades with their airy arcades and loggias (open daily Apr–Oct 9am–7pm; Nov–Mar 9am–5pm). Erected over an older Byzantine-style castle, the present 14th–15th-century Flamboyant Gothic building fronts the piazzetta and the basin. It is open to the public and audio guides are available at the entrance.

Where the *palazzo* joins the basilica's southernmost flank is the **Porta della Carta** (Gate of the Paper, where the doge posted

---

It's a Doge's Life

The doges saw their authority wax and wane from absolute monarch to pathetic figurehead. Subject to the changing powers of the republic's oligarchic council, many were murdered, executed for treason, or ritually blinded – traditional punishment for a disgraced ruler. Though elected by the council, many created virtual dynasties. When the revered Giustiniani family were reduced by battle and plague in the 12th century to one last monk, he was hauled out of his monastery on the Lido and persuaded to sire nine boys and three girls to continue the line before being allowed to return to his vows of chastity.

his decrees and scribes gathered). The Gothic sculpture shows the doge kneeling before St Mark's lion

In the inner courtyard the **Scala dei Giganti** staircase is so named for Sansovino's giant statues of Neptune and Mars. Visitors take the golden **Scala d'Oro** past the doge's opulent private apartments to the spectacularly decorated council chambers on the third floor. Here, as in most of the city's palaces and churches, the walls are decorated with painted panels and canvases by Venetian masters rather than frescoes, too easily damaged by the Venetian climate. Look out for Veronese's *Rape of Europa* and Tintoretto's *Bacchus and Ariadne* and *Vulcan's Forge* in the **Anticollegio**; a masterly allegorical series by Veronese glorifying Venice in the **Sala del Collegio**, where foreign ambassadors were received; and weapons and suits of armour in the **Armoury** *(Sala d'Armi)*.

Sculpture depicting Adam in the Garden of Eden, Doge's Palace

Highlight of the palace tour, back down on the second floor, is the huge **Sala del Maggior Consiglio** (Great Council Hall), where ordinary citizens presented their complaints in person in the republic's most democratic days before the oligarchy reserved it for their secret deliberations. The last doge presented his abdication to Napoleon here. Of the 76 doges portrayed, one is blackened out, Marino Faliero, beheaded for treason in 1355. Tintoretto's *Paradise* adorns the entrance wall above the doge's throne. Said to be the world's largest oil painting, 22 x 7m (72 x 23ft), it was done, with the help of son Domenico, when the

The Bridge of Sighs

artist was 70. Look for the brilliant colours of Veronese's oval ceiling painting of *Venice Crowned by Victory*.

Bridge of Sighs and the Prison

For those hoping to go from the sublime to the sinister, the palace **prisons**, neat and tidy today along their narrow corridor, become all too romantic with their 17th-century baroque **Bridge of Sighs** *(Ponte dei Sospiri)*. The celebrated passage linked the Ducal palace with the prisons, and those on their way to the torture chambers were supposedly moved to sigh. Original graffiti can be seen in the prisons, one of which held Casanova for 15 months in 1755 before he escaped.

There are guided tours to the lesser-known areas of the palace – *Itinerari Segreti* (Secret Itineraries) – in English (Apr–Oct daily at 9.55am, 10.35am and 11.35am; during other months check times of English-language tours, tel: 041 271 5911).

The waterfront **Riva degli Schiavoni** (Quay of the Slavs) begins at the Ducal Palace and is named after the Dalmatian merchants who unloaded their goods here. The ghosts of Dickens, Wagner and Proust wander around the lobby of the venerable **Danieli**, a former doge's residence and one of Italy's most romantic hotels. The lobby bar offers a moment of rest for the weary.

Probably nowhere is there so much spectacular painting on view in such a tiny space as in the **Scuola di San Giorgio degli Schiavoni** (open Tues–Sat 9.30am–12.30pm and 3.30–6.30pm, Sun 9.30am–12.30pm). This building was the confraternity guildhall of the wealthy *schiavoni* merchants who commissioned Vittore Carpaccio (whose parents belonged to the community) to decorate their hall. His nine pictures, completed between 1502 and 1508, cover the walls of the ground-floor chapel. Note the ornate wooden ceiling. It is one of a number of *scuole* (literally, 'schools' or confraternities) unique to the days of the Venetian Republic.

Just four minutes by *vaporetto* from the *piazzetta*, on its own little island, is the church of **San Giorgio Maggiore** (open daily 9.30am–12.30pm and 2.30–6pm); its campanile offers the most photogenic view of the city and lagoon. The 16th-century church is a rare ecclesiastical building by Andrea Palladio, the master Renaissance architect from nearby Vicenza whose classic designs have dominated aristocratic residential architecture throughout North America and Europe. His customary Corinthian-columned elegance prevails here, extended from the façade to an airy interior. Two superb paintings by an elderly Tintoretto flank the main altar, *Gathering of the Manna* and an otherworldly *Last Supper*, in which Jesus administers communion while servants bustle to clear up the dishes. The resident monks still offer Mass sung in Gregorian chant every Sunday. A lift ascends to the top of the belltower for super panoramic views.

Around the Accademia

With justifiable pride, the rambling **Galleria dell'Accademia** (Accademia Gallery; open Mon 8.30am–2pm, Tues–Sun 8.15am–7.15pm – times do vary) is devoted almost exclusively to the artistic legacy of the master artists of Venice and the Veneto, from the 14th century of the republic's emerging glory to the 18th century of its gentle decadence. One of Italy's most important art museums, showcasing the world's finest collection of Ventian art, it offers the chance to see just how little Venice has changed over the centuries. Here are a few of its most representative highlights:

Room 1: Dedicated to Byzantine and Gothic artworks including the 14th-century *Coronation of the Madonna* of Paolo Veneziano, first of the city's great masters, glowing with characteristic Venetian colour and texture.

Room 2: Giovanni Bellini, youngest and most gifted member of the painter family, brings gentle humanity to his *Enthroned Madonna with Job and St Sebastian* (1485).

Room 4: Andrea Mantegna (a brother-in-law of the Bellini family) shows why *St George*, the dragon-killer, became the most appropriate patron saint for England.

Room 5: Giorgione's *Tempest* (1505) is one of the museum's most cherished, most mysterious treasures – a girl calmly nursing her child in a landscape prickling with the electricity of the approaching storm. This room contains the most celebrated works.

Room 10: this is the most important of Renaissance rooms. Titian's *Pietà*, a vibrant last work completed by pupil Palma il Giovane, was originally intended for his tomb in the Frari church *(see page 131)*; Veronese's *Feast in the House of Levi*

Giorgione's *Tempest*

was meant to be the *Last Supper*, until the Holy Inquisition complained about its 'buffoons, drunkards, dwarfs, Germans and similar vulgarities'; Tintoretto gives full play to his dark sense of drama in the *Miracle of St Mark*.

Room 17: Canaletto's immensely popular 18th-century *vedute* (views) of Venice were aristocratic precursors of modern postcards; in such fine works as *Island of San*

Tintoretto's *Miracle of St Mark*

Giorgio Maggiore, Francesco Guardi managed to achieve both poetry and melancholy.

Room 20: Gentile Bellini breathes little life into his *Procession on San Marco* (1496), but it remains one of the museum's most fascinating 'photographs' of Renaissance Venice.

Room 21: Vittore Carpaccio depicts in nine canvases the bizarre *Story of St Ursula*, a British princess, said to have led 11,000 virgins on a pilgrimage to Rome, all of whom were raped and slaughtered on their way back.

Peggy Guggenheim Collection

To the east of the Accademia along the Grand Canal, a breath of the 20th century awaits at the **Peggy Guggenheim Collection** of modern art in the Palazzo Venier dei Leoni (open Wed–Fri and Sun–Mon 10am–6pm, Sat in June and July 10am–10pm). Home of the American heiress until her death in 1979, this unfinished 18th-century palace provides a delightful canal-side setting for what is widely considered one of the world's most comprehensive collections of modern art. Works include those by Picasso,

Santa Maria della Salute

Duchamp, Magritte, Kandinsky and Klee, Chagall, Dalí, Bacon and Sutherland, but it is known above all for Jackson Pollock, Mark Rothko and Robert Motherwell. In the garden are sculptures by Giacometti, Henry Moore and the collector's husband, Max Ernst. Guggenheim and her dogs are buried here. Behind the gardens are a gift shop and lovely café (limited menu).

Where the Grand Canal empties into the lagoon stands the imposing church of **Santa Maria della Salute** (open daily 9am–noon and 3pm–5.30pm). Called *'La Salute'* by the Venetians, Santa Maria is the masterpiece of Baldassare Longhena, built to mark the city's deliverance from a plague in 1630. For a baroque edifice, the interior is rather sober, even chaste. One of Tintoretto's best, the *Marriage at Cana*, is opposite the entrance, while three vivid Titian canvases decorate the chancel: *Cain and Abel*, *Abraham Sacrificing Isaac* and *David and Goliath*, their drama heightened by the perspective *di sotto in su* (looking up from below).

To the west of the Accademia, the **Ca' Rezzonico** (open Wed–Mon 10am–6pm, till 5pm in winter) is another canal-side design of Longhena, completed in the 18th century and now a museum of 18th-century life **Museo del Settecento Veneziano** dedicated to those swan-song years of Venice's Most Serene Republic, **La Serenissima**. When the last of the wealthy Rezzonico family disappeared, Elizabeth Barrett and Robert Browning bought the *palazzo* and the poet died in a first-floor apartment in

1889. The extravagant ballroom and soaring allegorical frescoes such as Giambattista Tiepolo's *Merit between Virtue and Nobility* in the 'Throne Room' (it's actually used for Rezzonico weddings) and others, more wistful, by Guardi all catch the tone of a declining Venice and the frivolous lives of the idle rich.

The Scuole of Venice

Venice was home to a number of *scuole* that were not 'schools' at all but old, secular confraternities similar to today's Freemasons, Rotarians, Elks or Lions. North of Ca' Rezzonico, the **Scuola Grande di San Rocco** (open daily Easter–Oct 9am–5.30pm; Nov–Easter 10am–4pm), is Venice's richest confraternity, in a fine 16th-century chapter house next to its own church. Local master Tintoretto (1518–94) won a competition to create some 50 paintings (the largest collection of his work) over 23 years. In the Sala Grande is the high drama of *Moses Striking Water from the Rock* and a fascinating *Temptation of Christ*, with Satan portrayed as a beautiful youth. Tiepolo and Titian are interlopers here, the latter with a solitary but remarkable easel painting of the *Annunciation*. Tintoretto's chiaroscuro masterpiece is the grandiose *Crucifixion* in the Sala dell'Albergo.

Nearby is the immense brick and white-marble Gothic Church of the **Frari** (full name *Santa Maria Gloriosa dei Frari*, built by the Franciscans; open Mon–Sat 9am–6pm and Sun 1–6pm), above all celebrated for the high altar adorned with Titian's jubilant *Assumption of the Virgin*. The master's only painting on such a massive scale is a triumph of primary reds, blues and yellows that irresistibly draw you up to the altar. Drag yourself away to see his other work here, the *Madonna di Ca' Pesaro* (left nave), in which St Peter presents Mary to the Pesaros, a wealthy local family. Venetian composer Monteverdi's tomb is in a chapel left of the altar. Titian died in 1576 during a plague and his monumental tomb is in the right aisle. Donatello has sculpted a fine polychrome wood *St John the Baptist* for his compatriots' **Florentine Chapel**, to the right of the altar. This is the largest and greatest of all of the Venetian Gothic churches.

The Rialto Bridge

Back on the Grand Canal: Longhena's baroque **Ca' Pesaro** is now the town's Modern Art Gallery (open Tues–Sun 10am–6pm, till 5pm in winter), devoted principally to a small collection of purchases from the Venice Biennale exhibitions. Italian artists – Futurists Giovanni Fattori and Telemaco Signorini and the Ferrara trio of Filippo de Pisis, Carlo Carrà and Giorgio de Chirico – are well represented; less so other Europeans, although there are works by Matisse, Klee and Ernst. The building also holds the Oriental Museum (open Tues–Sun 10am–6pm, till 5pm in winter).

Around the Rialto

The Rialto is the ancient commercial heart of the city, named after the 9th-century settlement on *Rivo Alto,* the high bank. Here, the Oriental spices and silks and exotic cargo from faraway ports were unloaded from the republic's ancient galleons. The merchants headed for the banks, the sailors to the brothels. Today, the action is in the food markets and boutiques on the Grand Canal's west bank. The **Pescheria** (fish market) bustles early in the morning except Sunday and Monday, while the **Erberia** (fruit and vegetables) is open until late afternoon. Hidden among it is the 11th-century church of **San Giacomo di Rialto** – San Giacometto to the locals who claim it to be the town's oldest.

The 16th-century **Rialto Bridge**, one of three that cross the Grand Canal, is an architectural icon designed by Antonio da Ponte for a competition entered by Michelangelo, Palladio and Sansovino. It's still one of the liveliest spots in town.

Northeast of the bridge, past the Fondaco dei Tedeschi post office, seek out the little 15th-century church of **Santa Maria dei**

Miracoli (open Mon–Sat 10am–5pm, Sun 1–5pm). Its refined façade of inlaid coloured marble and intricately carved friezes has won it the name of 'golden jewel box' *(scrigno d'oro)*, its local designer Pietro Lombardo being more sculptor than architect. Recently restored, this church is a favourite with Venetian brides.

Santi Giovanni e Paolo

It's worth carefully mapping out your visit to the **Campo Santi Giovanni e Paolo**. Follow the Calle Larga Giacinto Gallina to the humpbacked Ponte del Cavallo bridge for the all-important first view of the *piazza*'s magnificent **equestrian statue** of the *condottiere* Bartolomeo Colleoni by Andrea Verrocchio. Colleoni left his fortune to Venice on the understanding that his monument would be on Piazza San Marco. Once dead, he had to settle for this spot in front of the *Scuola* of San Marco, a clever Venetian solution. The *piazza*'s main attraction is the massive 13th-century Gothic church of **Santi Giovanni e Paolo** (open Mon–Sat 7.30am–12.30pm and 3–6.30pm, Sun 3–7pm), a name compressed by Venetians into San Zanipolo. Built by Dominicans, it was the doges' funeral church and there are many masterpieces among some 25 vast tombs.

Returning to the Grand Canal, you'll find in the glorious **Ca' d'Oro** (open Mon 8.15am–2pm, Tues–Sun 8.15am–7.15pm), the quintessential decorative tradition of Venetian architecture. Completed in 1440, its Gothic style bewitches you into imagining the long-gone gilt of its façade, from which it earned its name 'Palace of Gold'. Take a more leisurely boat-ride for the view from the canal. Treasures of Ca' d'Oro's **Galleria Franchetti** of Renaissance art include Titian's *Venus at the Mirror* and Mantegna's *St Sebastian*.

Evening light on the lagoon

Off the Beaten Track

The old **Jewish Ghetto** (northeast of the railway station) is particularly peaceful and reveals a fascinating page of Venetian history. It was the former site of an abandoned iron foundry – *ghetto* in old Venetian dialect – which lent its name to future enclaves throughout Europe. In 1516, some 900 Jews (rising to a peak of nearly 5,000 by the mid-17th century) were confined to what was then a remote and isolated island. They built the six- and eight-storey tenements you see today, twice as high as those permitted elsewhere, with some floors no more than 2m (6ft) high. Tours to the six still-active 16th-century synagogues are offered by the **Museo Ebraico** (daily except Sat 10am–6pm) in the Campo del Ghetto Nuovo.

The Islands

On the island of the **Giudecca**, you'll find another Palladio-designed church, the **Redentore** (open Mon–Sat 10am–5pm, Sun 1–5pm). The grace of its form is best viewed from across the canal,

Colourful houses on the island of Burano

because the dome disappears at closer quarters behind its elongated nave. The Giudecca is a quiet residential refuge popular with artists – and is home to some of Venice's most exclusive hotels.

Out in the lagoon, Venetians have been manufacturing glass on the island of **Murano** since 1292, when the hazardous furnaces were moved away from the city centre. Today, its factories and shops are an undeniable tourist trap, but the **Museo Vetrario** (Glass Museum: open Thur–Tues 10am–5pm, till 4pm in winter) tracing the glass industry back to Roman times is worth a look. The island's quiet spot is the 12th-century Venetian-Byzantine church of **Santa Maria e San Donato**.

The island of **Burano** is a simple fishing village and a tranquil haven, though the women making lace on the doorsteps of their colourful houses and artists on the quay are all but history. Much of the lace that's hawked is machine-made in China. The **Scula Museo del Merletto** (Piazza Galuppi, 187, open Wed–Mon 10am––5pm, till 4pm in winter) is devoted to the art of lace making.

The overgrown island of **Torcello**, beyond Burano, is one of the lagoon's oldest inhabited spots, prosperous until emptied by a malaria epidemic. Its cathedral, **Santa Maria dell'Assunta** (open daily 10.30am–6pm, till 4.30pm in winter), founded in the 7th century and rebuilt in 1008, is a splendid Venetian-Byzantine church.

With sandy beaches and smart hotels, the **Lido** is as restful as any fashionable seaside resort. After a couple of days in Venice, its cars come as something of a shock, although tourists and locals still prefer bicycles. Take tea in the Grand Hôtel des Bains to recall the decadent 1900s, evoked there by Thomas Mann's novella (and Luciano Visconti's movie) *Death in Venice*. A few public beaches are the principle draw in summer when heavy humidity can sap the energy of the most determined tourist.

The Veneto: the Venetian Mainland

The Venetian mainland reflects some of the *Serenissima's* artistic and architectural glories. Most of the cities remained under its domination until the 15th century, yet retained much of their individuality. An *autostrada* and easy train service link Venice to Padua, Vicenza and Verona for those in a hurry, but others should take the charming back roads; this is one of Italy's principal wine growing regions outside of Tuscany's Chianti area.

The Brenta Canal

When Venetian aristocrats gave up the high seas for a more leisurely life on the land, they built Palladian Renaissance villas and baroque country houses on the banks of the Brenta Canal between Venice and Padua.

Follow the canal along the pretty country road (route S 11) to Padua (Padova). First stop, off a side road to Fusina at Mira (about 20 km/12 miles from Venice), is Palladio's 1571 **La Malcontenta**, also known as **Villa Foscari** (open May–Oct Tues and Sat 9am–noon; other times by appointment; tel: 041 547 0012)), to which a too-flighty Venetian countess was sent to pine, malcontentedly. The villa, with a Classical portico to catch the summer breezes, was the Renaissance architect's 'visiting card' for scores of commissions, copied worldwide, especially on the cotton plantations of America's Deep South. At nearby Oriago, the Palladian style can be seen in **Villa Gradenigo** and at Mira, in the 18th-century **Villa Widmann**. The influence is clear even in the most spectacular of the Brenta villas, at Stra, the opulent **Villa Pisani** ◀ (Apr–Nov Wed, Fri and Sun 10am–noon and 3–6pm) or Villa Nazionale. Built for the Pisani doges in 1756, with 200 rooms, Tiepolo frescoes in the ballroom and a vast park with pond, labyrinth and stables, it was purchased by Napoleon in 1807 and subsequently hosted Tsars, Hapsburg emperors and, for their first meeting in 1934, Hitler and Mussolini.

A romantic way to visit villas on the Brenta Canal is by *burchiello,* a modern version of the rowing barge that took the gentry, Casanova and Lord Byron to their trysts and parties in the country. Get details from the city tourist office on the eight-hour trip, which goes in either direction on alternate days, optional return by bus, from March to October.

Padua (Padova)

This proud university town – Galileo taught physics here from 1592 to 1610 – was a major centre of the Risorgimento reunification movement. Something of the old spirit remains at the handsome Neo-Classical **Caffè Pedrocchi**, the activists' meeting place on a little square off bustling Piazza Cavour.

North along the Corso Garibaldi is Padua's undisputed draw, the 14th-century **Scrovegni Chapel** (open daily 9am–7pm). To see the frescoes it is essential to pre-book at least three days in advance (or 24 hours before with credit card, tel: 049 201 0020 or visit <www.cappelladegliscrovegni.it>. The chapel is also known, due to its site among ruins of a Roman amphitheatre, as the Arena Chapel. As a penance for his father's usury, the patrician Enrico Scrovegni built the simple little hall in 1303 specifically for the great Giotto frescoes. Beautifully preserved, these are considered some of the most important artworks of the early Renaissance. In 38 pictures arranged in three rows under a starry heavenly blue vault, Giotto tells the story of Mary and Jesus, movingly portrayed by the *Kiss of Judas*, the *Crucifixion* and the *Lamentation*. A monumental *Last Judgement* covers the entrance wall.

Giotto frescoes, Scrovegni

The entrance to Piazza del Santo south of the city centre is guarded by Donatello's grand **statue of Gattamelata**, the 15th-century Venetian *condottiere* Erasmo da Narni. Behind him is Padua's site of pilgrimage, the 13th- and 14th-century **Basilica di Sant'Antonio** (open daily 6.30am–7.30pm), the city's protector known simply as Il Santo, built in honour of the Portuguese-born Franciscan monk who died in Padua in 1231. The tomb of the patron saint of lost items is covered with photos, flowers and notes left by pilgrims.

Vicenza

This is the home town of Andrea Palladio (1508–80), the most important architect of the High Renaissance. At its centre, **Piazza dei Signori** is graced by Palladio's first public work, the **Basilica Palladina** (1549), a gathering place for the law courts and assembly hall of the Gothic Palazzo della Ragione that it encases with a colonnade and loggia (open summer Tues–Sun 10am–7pm; winter Tues–Sun 9am–5pm). Inside is a museum of Palladio's designs.

The main commercial street is **Corso Andrea Palladio**, lined with elegant mansions (converted to banks, shops and cafés) by the master and his disciples; his simple home was No. 163. The 15th-century **Palazzo da Schio** (No. 147) is also known as Ca'd'Oro, after the Venetian Gothic palace. Palladio's greatest opus is where the Corso widens into the Piazza Matteotti, giving him freedom for the airy **Palazzo Chiericati**. Its **Museo Civico** (open July–Aug Tues–Sun 9am–7pm and Sept–June 9am–4.45pm) has works by Tintoretto, Veronese and and Tiepolo.

Across the *piazza* in a little garden, the audacious **Teatro Olimpico** (open Sept–June Tues–Sun 9am–5pm; July– Aug Tues–Sun 9am–7pm) is Palladio's last work, completed by his protégé Vincenzo Scamozzi in 1584. Facing an amphitheatre auditorium are classical Roman statuary and columns that look far deeper than their 4m (14ft), a permanent stage 'curtain' of *trompe l'oeil* depicting the ancient streets of Thebes. It was the

> **'Basilica Palladina ranks among the most noble and most beautiful edifices since ancient times, not only for its grandeur and ornaments, but also its materials.'** That was Palladio's modest opinion of his own work.

first covered theatre in Europe and is still used.

Take route N 247 to Monte Berico and Palladio's most celebrated building, the hilltop **Villa Rotonda**, also known as **Villa Capra** (gardens open Mar–Nov Tues–Sun 10am–noon and 3–6pm; villa open Wed 10am–noon and 3–6pm), considered to be Palladio's finest work. Designed as a belvedere for Cardinal Capra in 1567, it's an exquisite piece of applied geometry, a domed rotunda set in a square surrounded on all four sides by simple Ionic-columned porticoes. From here it's a 10-minute walk to the Palladian-inspired **Villa Valmarana** (open mid-Mar–Nov Tues–Sun 3–6pm and till end of Sept Wed, Thurs, Sat and Sun 10am–noon), notable for its Tiepolo frescoes.

The Roman Arena in Verona

Verona

Shakespeare's 'Fair Verona' of *Romeo and Juliet* fame was first a favourite of ancient Roman emperors and the 'barbarian' rulers who followed. The city likes to be known as *la Degna*, the Dignified, but it also has a lively, well-to-do ambience, stimulated by the presence of its Adige river that flows down from the Dolomites.

The hub of city life is the vast Piazza Bra, with the town hall on its south side and the **Roman Arena** (Sept–June Tues–Sun 9am–6pm; July and Aug Tues–Sun 8am–3.30pm and Mon 1.45–7.30pm) dating to AD100. Only four of its outer arches survived an 1183 earthquake undamaged, but the inner arcade of 74 arches is intact. The amphitheatre's 22,000 seats sell out months in advance for open-air productions of the best-known operas such as *Aida*.

Along the north side of the Piazza Bra, the **Liston**, a people-watcher's delight lined with smart cafés and fine restaurants, is the street for the Veronese bourgeoisie's popular evening stroll *(passeggiata)*. It leads to the boutiques, galleries and antiques shops of the equally fashionable Via Mazzini. Turn right at the end down Via Cappello for the 13th-century *palazzo* that the local tourist authorities will have you believe was **Juliet's House** (*Casa di Giulietta Cappelletti;* open Tues–Sun 8.30am–7.30pm and Mon 1.30–7.30pm), complete with balcony. The **Piazza delle Erbe** along the ancient elongated Roman forum makes the prettiest of marketplaces and the adjoining, elagant **Piazza dei Signori** (also known as Piazza Dante) is ringed by crenellated *palazzos* and the historical Antico Caffé Dante. The 14th-century **Arche Scaligeri** (Scaligeri Tombs) just beyond are some of the most elaborate Gothic funerary monuments in Italy.

West of Piazza Bra, the massive brick 14th-century **Castelvecchio** (open Tues–Sun 8.30am–6.30pm) fortress on the Adige river now houses an art museum. Its collections are principally of the Venetian school, notably Mantegna's *Holy Family*, a Giovanni Bellini *Madonna* and Lorenzo Lotto's *Portrait of a Man*.

The austerely handsome 9th–12th-century basilica of **San Zeno Maggiore** (dedicated to the city's patron saint), is Verona's most visited church (open Mon–Sat 8.30am–6pm, Sun 1–6pm). The simple interior is illuminated by the magnificent Mantegna triptych (1459) on the high altar.

The Dolomites

The landscape of Italy's eastern Alps is a mixture of rich green Alpine meadows with jagged white limestone and rose-coloured granite peaks. Summer hiking in the largely German-speaking region of Alto Adige (Austrian South Tyrol till 1918) is a delight. Well-marked paths lead to farmhouses and rustic mountain restaurants where you can try the local cured ham *(Speck)* or spinach dumplings *(Spinatknödl)* as a change from pasta.

Bolzano (Bozen)

South Tyrol's historic capital makes a good base for walking. It has a 14th-century Gothic **church** with a characteristically Austrian polychrome tiled roof. The **Museo Archeologico** (open

The dramatic Dolomites

Tues–Sun 10am–5pm, Thur till 7pm) has a fascinating collection including the mummified body of Ötzi, found by chance in the Ötzaler Alps in 1991 and estimated to be over 5,000 years old. Head northeast of town to the **Renon** *(Ritten)* plateau for views of the Dolomite peaks, reached by cableway and funicular.

Cortina d'Ampezzo

The most upmarket of Italian winter-sports resorts, chic Cortina d'Ampezzo has elegant hotels, smart boutiques and a buzzing nightlife. In a sunny, sheltered basin high in the Boite valley of the eastern Dolomites, Cortina provides excellent skiing facilities and is also a favourite with summer hikers, many of whom come for guided treks in stunning scenery. Known as the 'Queen of the Dolomites', it is Europe's most beautiful alpine resort.

A series of three cable-cars link up to **Tofana** at 3,243m (10,640ft), from where there is a variety of walking (and skiing) trails linked by more than 50 mountain refuges/huts. The resort has over 25 mountain restaurants, most with fabulous views of the alpine scenery.

Emilia-Romagna

These two regions were united at the time of the 19th-century Risorgimento, with Emilia following the Apennines from Bologna to Piacenza, while Romagna covers the eastern area of Ravenna and the popular Adriatic resorts around Rimini down to Cattolica.

Rimini

The Adriatic coast, of which Rimini is the chief resort, has wide sandy beaches, at some points stretching 300m (1,000ft) from the water's edge back to the dunes. Its lively hotels, beach clubs and myriad discos make Rimini a favourite playground for sun-seekers (Germans, Scandinavians and Eastern Europeans arrive in droves) while in off-season months it is sleepy.

Inland, on the other side of the railway, is the old city that was Ariminium to the Romans. The 27BC **triumphal arch** *(Arco d'Augusto)* ornamented with medieval battlements stands at the junction of the imperial highways from ancient Rome: Via Flaminia and Via Emilia (which gave the region its name). The **Ponte di Tiberio** bridge built over the Marecchia river in AD14–21 is still in use. The unfinished 15th-century **Tempio Malatestiano** (open Mon–Sat 8am–12.30pm and 3.30–7pm, Sun 9am–1pm and 3.30–7.30pm) is an important Renaissance design of Leon Battista Alberti, incorporating elements of the Arco d'Augusto in the façade. More pagan temple than church, it served as a mausoleum for the cultivated but cruel tyrant, Sigismondo Malatesta and his wife, Isotta degli Atti.

Beach boys, Rimini

South of Rimini are the resorts of **Riccione** and (quieter) **Cattolica**. To the north is

Cesenatico, which is notable for its colourful fishing port.

Ravenna

The beautifully preserved mosaic decoration of Ravenna's churches, some 1,500 years old, come as an exciting revelation. They stand at the summit of the art as originally practiced by the Byzantines and are the finest in Europe.

Film director Federico Fellini, born in Rimini in 1920, immortalised the region in the 1970s with his Oscar-winning *Amarcord*. The Grand, the famous 'old lady' of Adriatic hotels, is beautifully located in the park named after Fellini.

Ravenna, now some 10 km (6 miles) from the sea, the capital of the Western Roman Empire after the fall of Rome was once a flourishing port. Honorius, last emperor of Rome, made it his capital in 404, but it was the Emperor Justinian in 540 who left his mark of Byzantine culture on the town.

You'll see something of the town's Venetian-dominated era on the graceful **Piazza del Popolo**, bordered by the 17th-century Palazzo Comunale. Next to the church of San Francesco, in a building from 1780, is the **tomb of Dante**, who died here, in exile, in 1321, with a fellow poet's epitaph: 'Here I lie buried, Dante, exiled from my birthplace, son of Florence, that loveless mother.'

The oldest, most striking of the Byzantine monuments, located in the northern corner of the city centre, is the 5th-century **Mausoleum of Galla Placidia** (open daily April–Sept 9.30am–6.30pm; Mar–Oct 9.30am–5.30pm; Nov–Feb 9.30am–4.30pm). Three sarcophagi stand in the cross-shaped chapel. The deep blue, gold and crimson mosaics on the vaults and arches depict *St Laurence*, *the Apostles* and the *Good Shepherd Feeding His Sheep* (over the entrance). These mosaics are the most beautiful of the era.

In the same grounds is the three-storey brick basilica of **San Vitale** (opening times as Galla Placidia), consecrated in 547. The octagonal construction provides the interior with seven *exedrae*, or recesses, the eighth being the choir and apse. The Old Testament scenes, such as *Abraham Sacrificing Isaac*, are more lively than the rigidly formal Emperor Justinian and Empress Theodora, with their court retinue and Christ between two angels, St Vitalis and, far right, Bishop Ecclesius holding a model of the church. These are the finest series of Byzantine mosaics outside Istanbul. The cloisters house a National Museum of Roman, early Christian and Byzantine Sculpture.

East of the city centre, the early 6th-century church of **Sant' Apollinare Nuovo** (open daily Apr–Sept 9am–7pm; Oct–Mar 9am–noon and 2–5pm) was built by the Christian Ostrogoth king Theodoric. In the nave, the church's famous Byzantine mosaics show, on the left, Ravenna's fortified port of Classis, from which a procession of 22 virgins follows the three Magi with gifts for Jesus; on the right, from Theodoric's palace, 26 male martyrs march towards Christ.

► Bologna

The capital of Emilia-Romagna is a thriving town with a certain patrician atmosphere to its beautifully preserved historic centre lined by 35 km (22 miles) of loggias, or arcade-covered sidewalks. It is famous as the home of Europe's oldest university, established in the 10th century on the foundation of a renowned law school dating back to the 5th century, the end of the Roman empire. The town's revered age-old place in Italian gastronomy compares to that of Lyon in France.

On the west flank of the **Piazza Maggiore**, the massive medieval **Palazzo Comunale** with a Renaissance porch is an expression of Bologna's civic power. The 14th-century basilica of **San Petronio** (open daily 7.30am–1pm and 2–6pm) ranks among the most imposing of Italy's Gothic churches. It has a fine **central portal** with reliefs of Old Testament scenes on its pilasters sculpted by Siena-born master Jacopo della Quercia. Adam's pose in the *Creation* scene (top left) inspired the Michelangelo figure reaching out to God on the Sistine Chapel ceiling.

In the adjoining square, the 16th-century **Neptune Fountain** is one of the town's most popular symbols, for which Giambologna sculpted the immodest bronze sea god surrounded by nymphs and cherubs. This scandalously proportional Neptune was once concealed (and protected) by bronze trousers.

A medieval atmosphere clings to the houses in the streets behind the Metropolitana Cathedral to the north. At the end of the Via Rizzoli, the two **leaning towers** are all that remain of a whole forest of over 200 medieval status-symbols. The Torre degli Asinelli (open summer daily 9am–6pm; winter till 5pm), 98m (320ft), is the taller, with 498 steps to its rooftop view. Built in 1109, it leans more than 2m (7½ft), less than its twin, Torre Giselda.

You'll find the city's characteristic arcaded *palazzi* along the Via Zamboni leading past the university to the **Pinacoteca Nazionale** (open Tues–Sat 9am–7pm). The gallery's fine collection is devoted largely to the Bologna school, most notably the baroque paintings of Guido Reni and the Carracci family, of whom Annibale is generally considered to be the most gifted.

South of the city centre, the founder of the Dominican order is buried in the basilica of **San Domenico** (open daily 8am–1pm

Bologna, capital of Emilia-Romagna

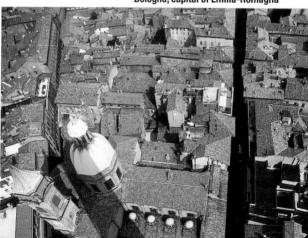

and 2.30–7.30pm), built in the 13th century with baroque modifications. The monk died in Bologna in 1221, and his **tomb** was designed later by Nicola Pisano with works by Nicolò dell'Arca and the 20-year-old Michelangelo – he did the saints Petronius and Proculus and the angel on the right – the first and last time he ever put wings on an angel.

Ferrara

A half-hour's drive from Bologna on the *autostrada* takes you to this stronghold of the high-living d'Este dukes – archetypally scheming, murderous, lovable Renaissance villains who ruled from 1200 to 1600. In their formidable (and recently restored) **Castello Estense** (open Tues–Sun 9.30am–5.30pm), a 14th-century moated fortress that is this lovely town's centrepiece, guides tell delightfully dubious tales of what went on in the dungeons.

You get a sense of the dukes' grandeur among the Renaissance *palazzi* of the **Corso Ercole I d'Este**, part of an ambitious 15th-century urban expansion, *Addizione Erculea*. The d'Estes' **Palazzo dei Diamanti** has 12,000 stones sculpted in the shape of a diamond on its walls and houses the **Pinacoteca Nazionale** (open Tues–Sat 9am–2pm, Sun 9am–1pm), with notable works of the Ferrara masters Cosmè Tura, Ercole de' Roberti, Garofalo and prints by Andrec Mategne. It also hosts visiting exhibitions.

The triple-gabled 12th-century **Cathedral** (open Mon–Sat 7.30am–noon and 3–6.30pm; Sun 7.30am–12.15pm and 4–7.30pm) still has its loggia of shops attached to the south wall. The cathedral museum exhibits two major works by Ferrara's 15th-century master Cosmè Tura, *St George* and the *Annunciation*, and sculptures by Jacopo della Quercia.

Parma

The home of two famous painters, Correggio and Parmigianino and birthplace of the conductor Arturo Toscanini, has much more to offer than just great cheese and ham. The **Piazza del Duomo** forms a harmonious space for the graceful baptistry, begun in 1196, and the austere nobility of the 12th-century

Cathedral (open daily 9am–12.30pm and 3–7pm), with its 13th-century campanile. Inside, on the ceiling of the central octagonal dome, are Correggio's greatest masterpieces, his **frescoes** of the *Assumption of the Virgin* (1530). Also acclaimed is Benedetto Antelami's *Deposition (Descent from the Cross)*. The 13th-century pink Verona marble **Baptistry** (open daily 9am–12.30pm and 3–6.30pm) has superbly sculpted doors by Antelami, who also carved most of the 12 statues of the months inside.

Behind the cathedral, the 16th-century Renaissance church of **San Giovanni Evangelista** (open daily 8am–noon and 3.30pm–6pm) also has in its dome a fine Correggio fresco of the *Vision of St John on Patmos*. Look for the Parmigianino frescoes in the first, second and fourth chapels on the left aisle.

In the lovely Benedictine **Monasterio di San Paolo** (Via Melloni; open daily 9am–1.45pm) is a private dining room *(Camera di Correggio)* for the unconventional abbess, Giovanna da Piacenza. She commissioned Correggio to decorate it in 1519 (his first work) with a feast for the senses, including mischievous *putti* and a view of Chastity as symbolised by the goddess Diana.

Frescoes in Parma Cathedral

The **Palazzo della Pilotta**, on Piazzale della Pace, is home to the Galleria Nazionale, housing work by Correggio and Parmigianino, the Biblioteca Palatina, Museo Archeologico and Teatro Farnese, a Palladian theatre with Italy's first revolving stage (all open Tues–Sun 8.30am–2pm).

THE NORTHWEST

Lombardy, Piedmont and the Ligurian coast make up the country's most prosperous region. Industry and commerce have made the fortune of its three great cities – Milan, Turin and Genoa. If the last has drawn on the riches of the seas, Milan and Turin, in close contact with France and Germany just across the Alps, have had the added underpinning of a flourishing agriculture in their Po Valley hinterland. The early lords of this constant economic expansion also called on the greatest artists both from Italy and beyond, from Leonardo da Vinci to Jan Van Eyck. The region has won world recognition in the vanguard of the arts, of modern design in clothes and furniture, not forgetting the automobile and communications industries.

For relaxation, the Italian Riviera east and west of Genoa alternates a rugged coastline with the occasional fine sandy beach. Hugging the slopes of Mont Blanc (Monte Bianco), Courmayeur is one of Italy's oldest and most picturesque ski resorts. North and east of Milan are the romantic lakes Como, Maggiore and Garda.

Milan

Quite happy to leave the embroiled politics of national government to Rome, Milan prides itself on being the country's economic, cultural and design capital. This is Italy at its most fashionable, self-assured and sophisticated. Yet despite its prestigious museums, excellent restaurants, shopping and magnificent Gothic cathedral, tourists do not think of Milan as an obvious holiday destination – though some do make the pilgrimage just for Leonardo da Vinci's *Last Supper*. But anyone interested in contemporary Italian life will want to experience its cafés and clubs, elegant shopping avenues and side-street art galleries.

Nowhere does a cathedral (the Duomo) more distinctly dominate a major city centre. Almost non-stop throughout the day, but especially in the evening, the time of the *passeggiata* (evening stroll), the **Piazza del Duomo** is one of the liveliest squares in Europe. It is dominated by the **Duomo** (open daily

The grandiose façade of Milan's Duomo

7am–7pm). The most grandiose of Italy's flamboyant Gothic cathedrals, it was begun in 1386 by the ruling Visconti family and involved teams of Italian, French, Flemish and German architects and sculptors. For the best view of that awesomely rich façade, completed in 1813, and a bristling silhouette of marble pinnacles and statues, stand in the courtyard of the **Palazzo Reale** south of the cathedral. (It houses the Cathedral Museum, which displays fine examples of sculpture from the façade.) The cathedral's interior is a vast space divided by 52 soaring columns and **stained-glass windows**, from the 15th century to the present day. The front of the Duomo is currently being restored, with the work expected to be completed in 2007.

Give yourself plenty of time for a spectacular walk out on the **roof** (open daily 9am–5.50pm; Feb–Nov till 4.50pm). The lift entrance (clearly signposted outside the cathedral) is in the right transept; alternatively, climb all 250 steps. Wander high above the city turmoil under the flying buttresses and around the statues (3,400 in all) and forest of pinnacles (135) for an unbeatable view of the city.

Information on ticket availability for La Scala productions is supplied by an electronic terminal next to the ticket office at the Duomo metro station. Payment in euros or by credit card. You can also phone the Scala Infotel Service, tel: 02 720 037 44, from 9am–6pm weekdays, and buy tickets by phone; tel: 02 860 775. Tickets can also be bought on the internet; <www.teatroallascala.org>.

Leading north from the Piazza del Duomo is the huge cross-shaped shopping arcade, **Galleria Vittorio Emanuele**, an impressive steel-and-glass monument to the expansive commercial spirit of the 19th century and a prototype of today's shopping mall. Cafés, restaurants, bookshops and boutiques are showcased here.

The Galleria provides a sheltered passage from the Duomo to another holy entity, the revered 18th-century **La Scala** theatre, high temple of opera. In January 2002, it closed for renovation, and reopened in December 2004. The **Opera House Museum** (*Museo Teatrale alla Scala;* open daily 9am–12.30pm and 1.30– 5.30pm) is now housed again at La Scala after its temporary home on Corso Magento. The museum traces the fascinating history of opera and theatre in the city, with memorabilia of composers including Verdi, Bellini and Donizetti on show as well as temporary exhibitions. You can also see the refurbished theatre from a box unless there is a rehearsal or production on stage.

Milan's most prestigious retail thoroughfare is **Via Monte Napoleone**, a parade of neoclassical *palazzi* and designer shops. The adjacent side streets, such as vias Borgospesso, Sant' Andrea, della Spiga and Bagutta, are also extremely upmarket.

Around Castello Sforzesco

The massive brick fortress, the **Castello Sforzesco** (open Tues–Sun 9am–5.30pm), situated northwest of the city centre, was built by the Visconti and rebuilt in its present form in the 15th century by Duke Francesco Sforza. The bulk of the solid square structure stands around a vast courtyard, Piazza d'Armiles. Beyond, in the handsome old residential quarters of the Corte Ducale, is the entrance to the Castello Sforzesco Musei Civici, a series of small **art museums** devoted to sculpture, painting *(Pinacoteca)*, ceramics, furniture and archaeology. In collections that include works by Giovanni Bellini, Mantegna, Titian, Correggio and Tintoretto, pride of place goes to Michelangelo's

Castello Sforzesco

last work (at the age of 89), the Rondanini *Pietà* (1564), now restored to its former gleaming white marble. He worked on until six days before his death, chiselling a strange throwback to medieval sculpture for his last tussle with the recalcitrant stone.

The Last Supper

Even without Leonardo da Vinci's masterpiece in the adjoining refectory, the church of **Santa Maria delle Grazie**, (Via Caradosso, southwest of the Castello; open Tues–Sat 7am–noon and 3–7pm Sun and holidays 7.30am–12.15pm and 3.30–9pm; times vary) would be worth a visit as a jewel of Renaissance architecture. Adding to an earlier Gothic design, Donato Bramante – Pope Julius II's chief architect in Rome – fashioned a magnificent red brick-and-white stone chancel *(tribuna)* in 1492. The graceful lines of the rectangular choir and 16-sided cupola are best viewed from Bramante's cloister built on the north side. Inside, stand in the choir to appreciate the dome's full majesty.

Leonardo da Vinci's ***The Last Supper** (Il Cenacolo;* tickets by reservation only, tel: 02 8942 1146, Mon–Fri 9am– 6pm, Sat 9am–2pm; operators speak English; book on <www.cenacolovinciano.org>) has been lovingly resuscitated in the Dominican refectory to the left of the church. The completion in 1999 of a laborious 20-year restoration helped remove centuries of deterioration and

Postmortem of a Masterpiece

The main culprit in the disintegration of the *Last Supper* was its creator, Leonardo da Vinci himself. For this summit of his life's work, he did not want the restrictions of fresco-painting onto damp plaster. A fresco, painted section by section without modifying once dry, would deny him the chance to add the overall shadowy *sfumato* effect that gave his paintings depth and subtlety. Nor would the sustained effort demanded by a fresco's damp plaster permit him, as was his habit, to leave the painting when inspiration deserted him, to go to work on something else.

So Leonardo chose to use a tempera with oil and varnish on a dry surface. Deterioration was already noted in 1517, when Leonardo was still alive. By the time fellow artist Giorgio Vasari saw it a generation later, there was 'nothing visible but a muddle of blots'. It's a miracle that 400 more years of dust and smog have left anything at all, much of it finally rectified by a decades-long restoration completed in 1999.

clumsy restoration since it was completed in 1497. It unveiled the enormous psychological impact in Leonardo's depiction of the trauma for each of the disciples when Jesus declares, 'One of you will betray me.' As a result of the painstaking recovery of the 'real' Leonardo, we can now see that Philip (third to the right) has an expression of acute grief rather than the simpering pathos left by 'restorers', who presumed to improve on the original.

For another aspect of Leonardo da Vinci's talents, visit the **Science Museum** (*Museo della Scienza e della Tecnologia Leonardo da Vinci;* open Tues–Fri 9.30am–5pm, weekends 9.30am–6.30pm), in a former Benedictine monastery on nearby Via San Vittore. The history of science and technology covers 28 sections, from astronomy to information technology with more than 15,000 exhibits. One gallery is reserved for Leonardo's inventions, displayed as models constructed from his notebooks. You'll see his aircraft, a machine for making screws, hydraulic timber-cutter, revolving bridge, various machine-tools and a system of map-making by aerial views.

At the eastern end of Via San Vittore, the imposing church of **Sant' Ambrogio** (open daily 8am–noon and 2.30–6pm; museum open daily 10am–noon and 3–5pm; except June–Sept closed Mon and Oct–May closed Tues) is the city's most revered sanctuary, built from the 9th–12th century. It stands on foundations that date to the time of St Ambrose (340–397), first bishop of Milan and a founding father of the Church; his remains are on view in the crypt. Its five-bayed façade set the gold standard for the Lombard Romanesque style.

Bellini's *Madonna and Child*, Pinacoteca di Brera

The Brera and Other Museums

The handsome 17th-century palace of the Jesuits contains the **Pinacoteca di Brera** (open Tues–Sun 8.30am–7.15pm), one of the country's foremost art museums of medieval and Renaissance art, concentrating on the master artists of northern Italy. A bronze statue of Napoleon (unusually, in the nude) stands in its arcaded courtyard. He was responsible for turning the Brera into a national gallery with confiscations from the Church and recalcitrant nobles. Among the museum's highlights are: two paintings by Giovanni Bellini of the *Madonna and Child*; Veronese's *Jesus in the Garden*; Tintoretto's *Discovery of St Mark's Body*; *Christ at the Column* by Donato Bramante; Mantegna's *Dead Christ*; and Raphael's *Mariage of the Virgin*. Non-Italian artists include El Greco, Rubens, Van Dyck and Rembrandt. In the modern collection, look out for Modigliani, Boccioni, de Chirico and de Pisis. The building is also home to Milan's art academy.

Brera is Milan's 'Greenwich Village'. It has been re-gentrified in the last decades and offers cutting-edge style and character in its trendy boutiques, stylish cafés and reputed art galleries.

The **Pinacoteca Ambrosiana** (Piazza Pio XI; open Tues–Sun 10am–5.30pm) has reopened in the restored 17th-century palace and library of Cardinal Federigo Borromeo. Its principal treasure, though of contested provenance, is Leonardo da Vinci's luminous *Portrait of a Musician* (1485). You can see his pervasive influence on Milanese artists in the decorative paintings of Bernardino Luini and a fine *Portrait of a Young Woman* by Ambrogio de Predis. Caravaggio's only still life, *Basket of Fruit*, is here.

The **Poldi-Pezzoli Museum** (Via Manzoni 12; open Tues–Sat 10am–6pm) is a small, formerly private collection displayed in its original home, dedicated to the city in 1881. The prize pieces of include Piero della Francesca's *San Nicola da Tolentino*, Mantegna's *Madonna and Child*, a Botticelli *Madonna* and Antonio Pollaiuolo's *Portrait of a Young Woman*. There are also decorative arts items on show, from clocks to sundials, glass and furniture.

Around Lombardy

The central part of the Po Valley is only a fraction of the Italian lands conquered by the Lombards when they crossed the Alps from eastern Europe in the early Middle Ages. But it proved to be the most fruitful, all too tempting to the acquisitive appetites of France, Spain and rival Italian duchies and city-states such as Venice, which pushed its Serene Republic as far west as Bergamo. Natural fertility was enhanced by Europe's most advanced systems of irrigation, still operating in the medieval canals that you'll see on your way south to Pavia. Lombardy's rice, wheat and corn are the basis of the nation's risotto, pasta and polenta.

On a more sentimental note, Italy's Lake District at the foot of the Lombardy Alps – its major lakes are Como, Garda and Maggiore – is the perfect setting for mending broken hearts, breaking mended hearts and all romantic conditions in between.

Village scene in Lombardy

Pavia

The Lombards' first capital, before Milan, is now a redbrick university town. Its main attraction, the spectacular **Charterhouse** or **Certosa di Pavia** (open Tues–Sun May–Sept 9–11.30am and 2.30–6pm; Oct–Mar till 4.30pm; Apr till 5.30pm), is in fact 10 km (6 miles) north of the city, a 30-minute drive from Milan. Built by the powerful Gian Galeazzo Visconti, Duke of Milan, as his family's burial chapel, the Carthusian monastery's 15th-century church is a high point in the transition from Flamboyant Gothic to Renaissance. The multi-coloured marble façade makes an impact, with statues of prophets, saints and apostles above the medallion reliefs of Roman emperors.

The massive Gothic interior is lightened by the brightly coloured paving and groin-vaulting. Among the chapels that were given baroque finishings in the late 16th century is an exquisite Perugino altarpiece of *God the Father*. In the right transept is the Visconti tomb and a door leading to the lovely small cloister of russet terracotta, with a fine view of the church's galleried octagonal tower. Since 1947, Cistercians

Santa Maria Maggiore, Bergamo

have taken over from the Carthusian monks and they continue to manufacture Certosa's well-known Chartreuse liqueur and herbal soaps, sold in an adjoining shop.

Bergamo

Rising out of the plain of the Po Valley on a steep little hill, 47 km (29 miles) east of Milan is the delightful town of **Bergamo**. The city has a proud soldiering history, giving the Venetian Republic a famous *condottiere*, Bartolomeo Colleoni, and the largest contingent in Garibaldi's 1,000 Red Shirts. The pleasant **Città Bassa** (lower city) at the foot of the hill is the attractive, modern town full of shops, hotels and restaurants known for a savoury risotto dish. **Piazza Matteotti** is the hub of a lively café scene. Opposite is the **Teatro Donizetti** and a monument to the opera composer who was born here in 1797 – accompanied by the naked lady he is said always to have needed for inspiration.

One of Italy's finest, **Pinacoteca dell'Accademia Carrara** (open Tues–Sun, 10am–1pm and 2.30–5.30pm), has an important Mantegna *Madonna and Child* and interesting works by Lotto (a Venetian master who lived in Bergamo for many years), Bellini, Raphael, Titian and foreign masters.

Venetian ramparts protect the historic **Città Alta** (Upper City) on the hill, the older section of town linked to the Città Bassa by funicular. The gracious **Piazza Vecchia** is surrounded by Renaissance public edifices, notably the **Palazzo della Ragione**. The town's most venerable building is the 12th-century Romanesque basilica of **Santa Maria Maggiore** (open daily 9am–12.30pm and 2.30–6pm; closed Mon afternoon; till 5pm in winter). Adjacent to the church is the Renaissance **Colleoni Chapel**, with ceiling frescoes by Tiepolo.

The Lake District

There are five major lakes in the Lake District, each with its own character. A playground of the rich, it has ravishing scenery and, in spite of its proximity to the Alps, a moderate climate.

Lake Garda (Lago di Garda)

Gaspare Bertolotti, regarded as the originator of the violin, is supposed to have based his design on the west shore of **Lake Garda**.  But Italy's largest and easternmost lake is shaped more like a banjo, 52 km (32 miles) from the rugged cliffs of the neck down to its broad 'sound box', 18 km (11 miles) across, surrounded by rolling green hills and gardens. The lake has bewitched lovelorn Roman poets, writers, artists and not a few modern celebrities. Graced with vineyards (notably Bardolino), lemon trees, olive groves and cedars, it has mild winters and mellow summers.

At the south end, boat cruises start out from Peschiera, Sirmione and Desenzano, recommended for its dramatic view

Road with a view along Lake Garda

Sirmione's moated castle

of the mountains. Begin your road tour out on the narrow **Sirmione** promontory. This former fishing village and renowned spa is the most popular of Garda's towns with a splendid view of the lake from the tower of the 13th-century moated castle, the **Rocca Scaligera**.

The winding **Gardesana Occidentale**, which cuts through the cliffs of the west shore, is a spectacular drive. **Gardone Riviera** is much appreciated for its parks and botanical gardens and as a base for walks back into the hills. Above the resort, in Gardone di Sopra, is a 20th-century 'folly', **Il Vittoriale** (daily Apr–Sept 8.30am–8pm; Oct–Mar 9am–5pm), the bizarre hillside residence of Gabriele D'Annunzio – poet, adventurer and fascist – who died here in 1936. Gardens of laurel and cypress lead up to a hilltop mausoleum of the writer's sarcophagus flanked by those of his disciples. It overlooks the prow of a patrol boat D'Annunzio commanded in World War I, the *Puglia*.

Lake Como (Lago di Como)

Embraced by green wooded escarpments and backed by the snow-capped Alps, **Lake Como** was favoured by some of England's most romantic 19th-century poets – Wordsworth, Shelley and Byron – and has a wistful atmosphere for the leisure hours of the Milanese (it's less than an hour from Milan). As at Garda, a mild climate nurtures luxuriant vegetation in the villa gardens and parks.

The lake dramatically divides into two arms on either side of the jewel of **Bellagio**, which juts out on a promontory. Up on the heights above the town, the elegant 18th-century **Villa Serbelloni** (open Tues–Sun guided tours 11am–4pm) stands in the middle of a lovely park of roses, camellias, magnolias and pomegranates. Run by the Rockefeller Foundation, its famous gardens can be visited by guided

Lakeside dining

tour. Don't confuse the Villa Serbelloni with the luxury lakefront hotel of the same name.

The lake's southwest arm is the most attractive for excursions. From **Lezzeno**, take a boat cruise to see the colourful grottoes and look out for the waterfall at Nesso. **Como** itself is a large factory town famous for its silk production, and it has a handsome Gothic-Renaissance cathedral, the **Duomo** (open daily 7am–noon and 3–7pm), crowned by a superb baroque dome added in 1744 by Turin's Filippo Juvarra. It stands next to the arcaded and half-timbered Broletto, 13th-century seat of municipal government.

The western shores of the lake are lined with gracious villas nestling in perfumed gardens. At **Cernobbio**, the 16th-century Villa d'Este is a palatial 5-star hotel, one of Europe's most special. Come at least for tea or a stroll among the cypresses and magnolias. Between the genteel resort towns (and ferry stops) of Tremezzo and Cadenabbia, you'll find one of the lake's most beautiful and famous residences (open to the public), the 18th-century **Villa Carlotta** (open daily 9am–6pm). There's a marvellous view of the lake from its terraced gardens, much visited for the display of camellias, rhododendrons and azaleas in late April and May.

Lake Maggiore

The northern, more blustery end of **Lake Maggiore**, the second largest after Garda, is in Switzerland, but the Italian side shares the other lakes' mellow climate known to the Romans as *Lacus Verbanus* (beneficient). The resort towns offer excellent opportunities for relaxation and sports, but for short visits you'll get a better idea of the lake aboard a boat cruise (3–4 hours, with a meal on board, from Stresa, Baveno or Pallanza) than by road.

Stresa is Maggiore's principal resort. The lakeside promenade, Lungolago, is famous for its flowers and bewitching view of the lake's islands. Take the cable car to the 1,491m (4,89 ft) peak of the **Mottarone** for an exhilarating view of the Lombardy lakes, the Alps and the Po valley. A toll road will also take you there via the Giardino Alpinia (Alpine Garden), which displays over 2,000 varieties of mountain plants.

The most popular boat trip from Stresa is to the **Borromean Islands** *(Isole Borromee)*, celebrated for their baroque *palazzi*

The Borromeos' 17th-century *palazzo* on Isola Bella

and magnificent gardens. They are still the property of the Borromeo family that provided Milan with its greatest cardinals. The 17th-century *palazzo* on **Isola Bella** (open daily mid-Mar–Oct 9am–5.30pm, till 5pm in Oct) is decorated with admirable paintings by Annibale Carracci, Tiepolo, Zuccarelli and Giordano. The terraced gardens are one of the finest ensembles of the Italian formal style. View the lake from the uppermost 10 terraces, by the unicorn statue that is the Borromeo family emblem.

Isola dei Pescatori (also known as Isola Superiore) is a peaceful fishing village with narrow streets, while **Isola Madre**, further out in the lake, is the largest of the islands

Piedmont *(Piemonte)*

This region of the fertile upper basin of the Po river lies in the foothills *(pied mont)* between the Appenines and the Alps at the French and Swiss borders. From the fall of the Roman Empire to the 19th century, it stood outside the mainstream of Italian history. Its royal House of Savoy walked a diplomatic tightrope between France, Switzerland, Spain and the German emperors until the fall of Napoleon. The new nationalism led Piedmont into the Italian orbit at the head of the Risorgimento movement, and the House of Savoy served as Italy's reigning royal family from 1861 to 1946, with Turin briefly capital of the newly unified Italy in 1861.

Turin *(Torino)*

Best known for its industry, most notably the giant Fiat and Pirelli works, the Piedmontese capital is far from a dismal factory town. It has retained the grid-like layout of its origins as Taurinorum, a Roman *castrum*. Its rise to prominence in the 17th and 18th centuries was accompanied by Italy's first coherent urban planning; classical and baroque palaces and monuments give its main streets and squares a great dignity and panache buoyed by the city's economic prosperity. It has also been chosen as the host city of the Winter Olympics in 2006.

The tone is set by the formal elegance of the **Piazza Castello**, dominated by Filippo Juvarra's richly articulated baroque façade for the **Palazzo Madama**, currently undergoing restoration (for free tours of the restored part, tel: 01 1442 9912). The medieval castle received its new name when transformed in the 17th century into the royal residence of Vittorio Amedeo I's widow, nicknamed 'Madama Reale', also known as Maria Cristina of France. It houses the **Civic Museum of Ancient Art** (*Museo Civico di Arte Antica*; closed for restoration till 2006).

Across the square is the former royal chapel, the 17th-century church of **San Lorenzo** (open Mon–Fri 7.30am–noon and 4–7pm; Sat till 7.30pm; Sun 9am–1pm, 3–7.15pm and 8.30–10pm), designed by Turin's great baroque architect, Fra Guarino Guarini. Philosopher and mathematician as well as priest, he has created an intricate interior surrounding the octagonal space. A replica of the shroud is on show here.

Turin's Piazza Castello

The ornate **Royal Palace** (*Palazzo Reale*; open Tues–Sun 8.30am–7.30pm) was the baroque home of the Savoy princes from the mid-1600s to 1865. After strolling through one lavish room after another, visit the wing that houses the **Armoury** (*Armeria Reale*), one of the most comprehensive in Italy. Then relax behind the Palazzo Reale in the **Royal Gardens** (*Giardini Reali*; open 9am–one hour before sunset), by French landscape-architect, André Le Nôtre.

The Turin Shroud

The late 15th-century **Cathedral** (*Duomo di San Giovanni Battista*; open Mon–Sat 7am–12.30pm, 3–7pm; Sun 8am–

12.30pm and 3–7pm) cherishes one of Italy's most celebrated (and controversial) relics, the **shroud** said to have wrapped Jesus after his descent from the cross, taking the imprint of his face and body. Sometimes enshrined in the **Chapel of the Holy Shroud** *(Cappella della Santa Sindone)*, it was brought to Turin in the 17th century after a journey 200 years earlier from Jerusalem to France via Cyprus. Measuring 4.1 by

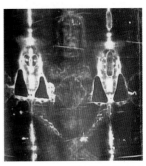

The Turin Shroud

1.4m (13 by 5ft), the sheet is kept in an iron-lined silver casket in a marble urn behind bullet-proof glass on the left-hand transept of the cathedral. Its next public appearance is scheduled for 2025. A copy, a third smaller than the original, is on view, however.

Many dispute the modern scientific tests that have proven it to be a medieval fabrication, and crowds of the faithful and merely curious still visit its black marble chapel, a masterpiece of Guarini's high baroque. It was restored after a 1997 fire when it came close to being completely destroyed. The **Museo della Sindone** (Via S. Domenico 28, open 9am–noon and 3–7pm) covers the history of scientific tests carried out on the cloth over the years.

However, the pride of Turin is not in one monument but in its royal palaces, baroque castles and churches, harmonious piazzas and sweeping boulevards that grace the city centre, covered by 18 km (11 miles) of elegant, colonnaded walkways. For the Torinesi, the city's heart is the elegant arcaded **Via Roma**, which is lined by the most exclusive shops and designer names. The Piazza Carignano was the city's political centre in the 19th century, and its palazzo was the seat of Italy's first parliament from 1861 to 1864. Nearby are some of the city's most important and fascinating museums and galleries, including the Egyptian Museum. The Piazza San Carlo, known as the city's 'drawing room', is home to beautiful baroque palaces, churches, elegant historic cafes and prestigious clothes shops.

The city's enduring symbol, the **Mole Antoniella**, from the top of which there are stunning views, houses the **Museo Nazionale del Cinema** (open Tues–Sun 9am–8pm, Sat till 11pm). The Italian film industry began in Turin in 1904, and this museum traces cinematic history from magic lanterns to cutting-edge technology.

Northeast of the *piazza*, in the Palazzo dell'Accademia delle Scienze, is the **Egyptian Museum** (*Museo Egizio*; open Tues–Sun 8.30am–7.30pm), second in importance only to the one in Cairo. The Savoys' collection of over 30,000 items is on display, while the second floor's excellent **Galleria Sabauda** (Savoy Gallery; open Tues, Fri, Sat and Sun 8.30am–2pm, Wed and Thur 2–7.30pm) has an important collection of Italian and European art.

Italy's automobile history – Fiat, Alfa Romeo, Bugatti and Ferrari – is celebrated at the **Museo dell'Automobile** (Corso Unità d'Italia, 40; open Tues–Sun 10am–6.30pm, and Thurs till 10pm), south of the city centre beside the Po river. It is near to the Lingotto, the original site of the first factory and now a huge entertainment complex with futuristic architecture on the roof.

Courmayeur

In 2006 Turin hosts the Winter Olympics, and most of the skiing and snowboarding events will be held in the three ski resorts, **Sestriere**, **Sauze d'Oulx** and **Bardonecchia** in the north of Piedmont, close to the French border. All part of the **Via Lattea** or "Milky Way" area, covering 400 km (250 miles) of slopes, **Sestriere** was the first purpose-built Alpine ski resort, created by Fiat baron Giovanni Agnelli. In the Valle d'Aosta, the pretty and chic town **Courmayeur** is framed by Mont Blanc (Monte Bianco) from where there are lovely walks, mountain climbing and good skiing in winter. On the northern side of the area the peaks of the Matterhorn (Monte Cervino) gaze down over **Breuil-Cervinia**, one of Italy's first ski resorts and still very popular. In the south of the region is Italy's first national park, the **Parco Nazionale del Gran Paradiso**, a haven of wildlife and beautiful scenery.

Quintessential Riviera: the harbour at Portofino

Aosta, the town from which the valley takes its name, was named after Emperor Augustus who created one of his mini-Romes in the centre of the valley. This attractive mountain town is encircled by the Alps and still has many Roman remains.

One of the most spectacular trips in Italy, with amazing views towards Mont Blanc, is the **cable car ride** from La Palud, north of Courmayeur, to the Colle del Gigante, at 3,354m (11,004ft), and Aiguille du Midi, at 3,842m (12,606ft), to Chamonix in France.

Italian Riviera

The Ligurian coast that holidaymakers have dubbed the Italian Riviera has an ancient history of piracy and commerce that are not always easy to tell apart. The great port city of Genoa made the Mediterranean more or less safe for respectable traders and the rest of the coast finally settled down to some quiet fishing, sailing and harmless traffic in postcards and suntan lotion.

The picturesque, more rugged coast east of Genoa is known as the Riviera di Levante (Riviera of the Rising Sun), while the coast west is the Riviera di Ponente (Riviera of the Setting Sun).

Genoa, birthplace of Columbus

Genoa (Genova)

Hemmed in between the Apennine mountains and the sea, Genoa, birthplace of Christopher Columbus, turned its back on Italy to seek its fortune on the high seas. With 28 km (17 miles) of docks, Italy's biggest port remains the key to the city's identity.

The main shopping street of this city, acclaimed as a European City of Culture in 2004, is Via XX Settembre west of the Piazza De Ferrari that constitutes the city's bustling modern centre, where the historic quarters begin. **Piazza San Matteo** was the home of the august Doria family, navigators and merchants who helped build Genoa's great commercial empire. Their arcade houses, with grey-and-white striped façades (Nos. 15–17) were built from the 13th–15th century. The church of **San Matteo** has the same grey-and-white façade. In the crypt, you'll find the tomb of Andrea Doria, great 16th-century admiral and city ruler.

At Via Garibaldi 11 **Palazzo Bianco** (open Tues–Fri 9am–7pm, Sat and Sun 10am–7pm) makes a sumptuous setting for the city's most notable art collection (mostly Genoese paintings). The 17th-century baroque **Palazzo Rosso** (No. 18; Tues–Fri 9am–7pm, Sat and Sun 10am–7pm) includes works by Veronese, Titian, Caravaggio, Dürer and Rubens.

Near the Porta Soprana is the **Casa de Cristoforo Colombo** (open Sat and Sun 9am–noon and 3–6pm) where the explorer is supposed to have spent his childhood. The house is, in fact, an 18th-century reconstruction. The harbour Expo site, created for the Columbus quincentennial anniversary of his 1492 voyage, includes Europe's largest **Aquarium** (Mon–Wed and Fri 9.30am–8.3pm, Sat and Sun 9.30am–10pm; closed Nov–Mar).

Riviera Resorts

Along the mostly rugged Riviera di Levante east of Genoa, by far the prettiest spot is tiny **Portofino**, seemingly more fishing and sailing harbour than resort, but look and you'll find some fine 'extremely exclusive' hotels and private villas back in the forest-covered hills. From the colourfully painted houses clustered around the postage stamp-sized harbour, avoid the crowds of day-trippers by setting out on a paved cliff walk. Pass the yellow-painted church of San Giorgio to the **Lighthouse** *(faro)* at the end of the government-protected Promontory Monte Portofino for a superb view along the coast. The cliffs are clothed in a profusion of exotic vegetation, with occasional glimpses of private homes framed by cypresses, palm trees and cascades of bougainvillaea. Boat excursions will take you to other beautifully secluded villages, such as the historic monastery of **San Fruttuoso**, reachable only by boat or a two-hour walk, and delightful **Camogli**. By foot, you can also visit the charming little fishing hamlet of **San Rocco** and take a 40-minute walk over to Punta Chiappa, looking out over the whole Riviera.

A favourite boat ride from Santa Margherita is to the cluster of former fishing villages called the **Cinque Terre** – cliff-clinging hamlets hugging a stretch of coastline reminiscent of the Mediterranean of one hundred years ago. Reachable only by boat until recently, they are linked by a network of ancient cliffside

Camogli

Carrara marble

mule paths that provide some of Italy's loveliest treks.

Santa Margherita Ligure is a lively resort town full of cafés, boutiques, good hotels and a palm-lined waterfront esplanade with seafood-serving *trattorie*. It absorbs the tourism neighbouring Portofino cannot accommodate. The family resort of **Sestri Levante** has fine sandy beaches. Most popular of all, down the coast beyond the naval city of La Spezia, are the beaches of **Viareggio**, a favourite Tuscan resort, together with its more up-market neighbour, **Forte dei Marmi**.

Cool off with an excursion inland to **Carrara**, where the marble quarries provided the raw material for the monuments of the Roman Empire and the Renaissance. The town is still full of sculptors and Piazza Alberica is the scene of a summer sculpture competition. Visit the still-active **quarries** of Fantiscritti and Colonnata; the marble that Michelangelo chose for his *Moses* and *Pietà* is now hewn at more than US$3,000 a cubic metre.

The Riviera di Ponente, west of Genoa towards the French border, is an almost continuous chain of family resorts. A faded resort of earlier times, dignified **San Remo** has a well-heeled casino and elegant promenade along the Corso Imperatrice. For time away from the beach, explore the narrow, winding medieval streets of the hilltop **La Pigna** quarter, leading up to the 17th-century sanctuary of Madonna della Costa.

The quieter resort of **Bordighera** is particularly proud of the palm trees along the Lungomare Argentina promenade. **Alassio** completes this coast's trio of major resorts, justifiably proud of its gardens nurtured by a particularly mild winter. An excursion east leads to the quiet medieval town of **Albenga**.

THE SOUTH

One of the great joys of the south is the extent to which it is still virgin land for the majority of Italy's visitors. It has its perennial favourites: the sister islands of Capri and Ischia in the Bay of Naples, the ruins of Pompeii, and the resorts of the singularly beautiful Amalfi coast. Otherwise, southern Italy is overlooked by tourists almost as much as it has been by the national government since the 1871 reunification.

Less prosperous than the north although benefiting from EU funds, it cannot offer the same wealth of modern hotel facilities. Monuments and museums have suffered from earthquakes and civic neglect. But things are slowly improving, and the compensations for the more venture-some visitor are considerable.

Positano on the Amalfi coast

The chief pleasure of the south, or Mezzogiorno, is the people, who are warm-hearted, outgoing and gregarious.

Naples *(Nápoli)*

The very idea of this teeming, undisciplined town once intimidated the faint-hearted, but the past decade has seen change in this history-rich city of which the enterprising and cheerful Neapolitans are justifiably proud. For adventurous travellers looking for an introduction to the south, the rewards are rich. Indeed, two of Naples' museums are among the most important in Europe, but they play second fiddle to the colourful street life.

Castel Nuovo

In the outdoor theatre that is Italy, Naples has unabashed melodrama to be seen everywhere: around the port, the popular quarters of Spaccanapoli, even the more bourgeois neighbourhoods of Vomero and Posillipo. You'll want to spend hours in the restaurants – this is where pizza began.

The face of Naples has been made and remade by its many earthquakes. Many churches, palaces and museums still show signs of ongoing reconstruction and restoration after the devastating quake of 1980.

The Port and Spaccanapoli

Traffic roars down the broad Corso Umberto I towards the pivotal **Piazza Municipio** to serve the docks or spin off into the commercial district behind Santa Lucia, the teeming historic centre of Spaccanapoli, or the residential districts of Vomero and Posillipo. Towering over the long rectangular square on its south side is the massive dry-moated **Castel Nuovo**. The 13th-century fortress of Naples' French ruler Charles d'Anjou, it was rebuilt in the 15th century as a palace for the Spanish kings of Aragon. Entrance to what is now administrative offices and a communal library is between two towers on the west side through a two-storey Renaissance **Triumphal Arch** crowned by a statue of St Michael.

The old popular harbour district of **Santa Lucia** is lined with elegant hotels and restaurants, many overlooking the formidable medieval **Castel dell'Ovo** (*Egg Castle*; open Mon–Fri 9am–6pm, Sat–Sun 9am–2pm) on an islet, with a handful of outdoor *trattorias* and cafés that enjoy a unique setting. The waterfront walk at sunset offers timeless views of the bay and Mount Vesuvius, with the addition of a gleaming-white cruise ship or two. At the workaday zone of Mergellina at the western end of the harbour, fishermen bring their morning catch into Porto Sannazaro.

South of the Piazza Municipio, the Via San Carlo curves round to the 19th-century steel-and-glass shopping arcade of **Galleria Umberto I**, opposite the great neoclassical temple of Neapolitan *bel canto*, the **Teatro San Carlo** opera house. Built in 1737 and rebuilt in 1816, it was once under the musical direction of Gioacchino Rossini (1815–1822) and has excellent acoustics. The monumental **Piazza del Plebiscito** was laid out by Joachim Murat, King of Naples, who occupied the Spaniards' **Palazzo Reale** (open Thur–Tues 9am–9pm) on the east side of the *piazza*. The rooms are decorated and furnished with the baroque pomp of the 17th and 18th centuries and reconstructed following Allied bomb damage in 1943. The *palazzo*'s sumptuous royal apartments are the draw, but it also holds temporary exhibits.

Galleria Umberto I

Leading north from the palace, the Neapolitans' favourite shopping street of **Via Toledo** separates the town hall *(Municipio)* and the broad commercial streets going down to the harbour from a chequerboard of narrow alleys to the west. This 16th-century Spanish neighbourhood, a mass of dilapidated working-class housing, is a great opportunity for watching everyday life. Via Toledo leads to the old historic heart of **Spaccanapoli** (around a Roman road that divides Naples into upper and lower districts). In an area stretching from the traffic-jammed Piazza

> **The cautious tell you not to drive in Naples, where one-way signs are meaningless, parking is impossible, traffic is relentless and red and green lights can be purely decorative. They are right.**

Dante, between Via San Biagio dei Librai and Via Tribunali and over to the Porta Capuana, the popular image of old Naples survives. A permanent festival of laundry hangs across the narrow streets. Gossip flies between balconies, while ropes haul up baskets of vegetables, letters and even pet cats.

Santa Chiara

For a sense of the historic neighbourhood's old splendour, start on **Piazza Gesù Nuovo**, with the extravagant baroque Immacolata column *(guglia)* in the centre. Architectural exuberance continues inside the Jesuit church. But the jewel, on the south corner of the square, is the 14th-century Gothic church of **Santa Chiara** (open daily 7am–12.30pm and 4.30–7pm), built for the wife of Robert the Wise d'Anjou and retrieved from its 18th-century baroque additions and 1943 firebombing. The rose window and elegant porch survive and the French Gothic interior is beautifully restored. Vaults include the **sculpted tombs** of Marie de Valois (on the right) and Robert the Wise d'Anjou (d. 1343; behind the high altar). Next to the church are the lovely 14th-century **cloisters** *(Chiostro delle Clarisse;* open daily 9.30am–1pm and in winter, also Mon–Sat 2.30–5.30pm*)*, converted in 1742 into a country garden of shaded walkways and Capodimonte tiles – a delightful haven and one of the city's most charming spots.

Take the Via Tribunali to the Franciscan church of **San Lorenzo Maggiore** (open daily 9am–1pm and 4pm–6.30pm; closes at 5.30pm in winter). Is baroque façade, incorporating a 14th-century marble porch, was added after the earthquake of 1731. Inside is a sober French Gothic chancel.

The three original 14th-century portals of the **Cathedral** (open Mon–Sat 8am–12.30pm and 4.30–7pm, Sun 8.30am–1pm and 5–8pm) are overpowered by the 19th-century neo-Gothic façade. It contains Naples' earliest-known Christian sanctuary, the 4th-century **Basilica of Santa Restituta**, in which the original Roman columns survived the 1688 earthquake. At the end of the right nave is the 5th-century domed baptistry, one of the oldest buildings in Europe, with some original mosaics intact. The cathedral's richly baroque **Chapel of San Gennaro** is the highlight. Its altar contains two phials of blood from Naples' patron saint and three times a year (the first Sunday of May, 19 September and 16 December) it is said to liquefy, or 'boil': When it fails, disaster befalls Naples. The last time it is said to not have liquefied was 1980, the year of the great earthquake.

The Museums

The roguish image of the city's present make it easy to forget its glorious past. Luckily, two truly magnificent museums preserve the region's treasures from the ravages of earthquake and theft.

View of Naples with the Bay and Vesuvius beyond

Constructed in the 16th-century as a cavalry barracks, the **Archaeological Museum** (*Museo Archeologico Nazionale*; open Wed–Mon 9am–7.30pm; closed Tues) is a feast of southern Italy's Greek, Etruscan and Roman past. All visits to Pompeii and Herculaneum should begin or end here, since the world-famous collections display not only the paintings and mosaics buried there by Mount Vesuvius nearly 2,000 years ago, but a host of other sculptures from the region's villas and temples.

The ground floor is devoted to **sculpture**, including many Roman copies of classics from Greece's Golden Age in the 5th century BC, which are our only access to these lost masterpieces. The most famous is the *Doryphorus* (Spear-carrier) of Polycletus, second in fame among Greek sculptors only to Phidias. Also on display is the **Farnese Bull** *(Toro Farnese)*, the largest classical sculpture ever discovered, hewn from a single marble block.

Most popular are the stunning **Herculaneum bronzes** and **Pompeii mosaics** on the mezzanine floor. The lively mosaics from

Mosaic of a chained dog, from Pompeii

Pompeii's patrician villas make a striking contrast with the rigid formality of church mosaics elsewhere in Italy. They include *Clients Consulting a Sorceress*, *Strolling Musicians*, vivid little friezes of an octopus, a chained dog, a cat catching a quail and the huge exciting mural of Alexander driving Darius of Persia from the battlefield at Issus in 333BC. The **paintings** here are the best preserved of any from Roman antiquity – frescoes in brilliant blues, greens and the inimitable Pompeii reds. The most celebrated is the sophisticated portrait of *Paquius Proculus and his Wife*. Also look for the elegant *Hercules and Telephus* and four delicate portraits of women, including *Artimedes* and *the Flower Gatherer*. Opened in 2000, the **Gabinetto Segreto** (Secret Gallery) displays a small but discerning collection of mosaics and paintings, many never before seen because of their controversial (some would say 'erotic', others 'pornographic') nature. The gallery can be visited by guided tour only, arranged upon the purchase of your ticket at the museum entrance.

Paintings in the Capodimonte Museum

The **Capodimonte Museum** (open Tues–Sun 8.30am–7.30pm; ticket office closes at 6.30pm) is housed in a beautifully restored 18th-century hilltop palace, the **Palazzo Realedi Capodimonte**. The grounds offer a welcome rest before and after a visit to the exceptional collection of Italian and European paintings. Highlights include: Giovanni Bellini's gentle *Transfiguration of Christ* standing serenely between Moses and Elijah; Mantegna's *Portrait of a Boy*; and Michelangelo's drawing of *Three Soldiers* for his Vatican fresco of *St Peter's Crucifixion*. The stark realism you'll see in Caravaggio's *Flagellation* and the *Seven Works of Mercy* launched a whole Neapolitan school of 'Caravaggeschi' shown here.

Vomero and Posillipo

Much of Naples' middle class looks out over the city from the hilltop Vomero neighbourhood. On the southeast edge of the hill just below the massive Castel Sant' Elmo, the elegant baroque charterhouse **Certosa di San Martino**, now home to the **Museo**

Nazionale di San Martino, (open Tues–Fri 8.30am–7.30pm; Sat–Sun 9am–7.30pm) offers a soothing haven of tranquillity in its cloisters and monastery gardens – and unbeatable views. The monastery's museum traces the kingdom of Naples' long history in costumes, sculpture, paintings and prints. A popular exhibition in the museum shows four centuries of the unique Neapolitan speciality of hand-crafted Nativity characters, known as *presepi*.

Campania

The fertile region around Naples, between the Tyrrhenian coast and the western slopes of the Apennines, was colonised by the Etruscans and Greeks. Since time immemorial, the volcanic soil has produced a profusion of olives, walnuts, grapes, oranges, lemons and figs. The succession of authoritarian rulers from the Middle Ages to the 18th century – Norman and Angevin French, German emperors and the Spanish – kept in place a feudal system that has left the region to this day socially backwards compared with the north. Village festivals and processions bear witness to the heavy rural attachment to religion and even pagan superstition harking back to ancient times. The international jetset has long frequented the idyllic islands in the Bay of Naples and the resorts of the Amalfi coast. In easy reach of Naples' museums are the archaeological remains of Pompeii and Herculaneum, the Vesuvius volcano and further down the coast, the Greek temples of Paestum.

Street card game

Capri

Ferries or hydrofoils leave from Naples, Sorrento and Positano (and Amalfi in the summer months only) for this fabled island 10 sq km (4 sq miles) in size. With walled villas surrounded by gardens, mountainous terrain and a very dramatic craggy coastline, this beautiful island manages to cater to the boisterous fun of day trippers and package tourists while providing quiet hideaways for pure hedonism. Winters here are marvellously mild and deserted, but even during the peak summer months you can seek out the island's many enchanted corners away from the crowds. Evenings are immeasurably calmer, when the local folk

Eternally popular Capri

venture out to reclaim the cafés and restaurants until the cool small hours and restore some of the charm and seduction for which Capri has been famous since the times of the ancient Roman emperors.

It's useless to apply for a special permit to bring your car, which is pretty much impossible (and unnecessary) during high season anyway. At the main harbour of Capri's **Marina Grande**, take a bicycle taxi, minibus or the funicular railway (the most practical) up to the main town of **Capri**. You can rent a taxi for the day – not cheap, but negotiable. Here, souvenir shops, pricey boutiques and bar-cafés cluster around the pretty 17th-century domed church of **Santo Stefano** in the Piazzetta (officially the Piazza Umberto I) where the funicular stops. Many day trippers see little more than this. Escape down the little road south of town to the peace of the shady cloisters of the 14th-century **Certosa di San Giacomo**, or in the direction of Via Camerelle that eventually leads to the famous Punta Tragara lookout and the **Faraglioni**. These rocky islets carved into fantastic shapes are a symbol of the island's beauty.

Dominating the western (and larger) side of the island, the quieter and only slightly less crowded hillside town of **Anacapri** derives a sleepy charm from its white villas along narrow lanes flowering with bougainvillea. A short walk from

Snow white church, Ischia

Piazza della Vittoria takes you to **Villa San Michele** (open May–Sept daily 9am–6pm; reduced opening in winter), home of Swedish doctor-writer Axel Munthe (d. 1949). The house is a mixture of baroque furniture and Roman antiquities, but the main attraction is the garden with dramatic views across the island and the bay. Back at the *piazza*, take the *seggovia* chairlift for a view of the island and some of the mainland on your way to the terraced gardens of **Monte Solaro**, at 589m (1,933ft), Capri's highest point.

The island's most popular excursion – prettiest by boat from Marina Grande, but also possible by road northwest of Anacapri – is to the celebrated marine cave, the **Blue Grotto** *(Grotta Azzurra)*, most effective (and crowded) at noon. The sun shining through the water turns the light inside the cave a brilliant, unearthly blue and objects on the white sand seabed gleam like silver. The cave, 54m (177ft) long, 15m (49ft) high and 30m (98ft) wide, is believed to have been a *nymphaeum*, a kind of watery boudoir for the Emperor Tiberius, who retired to Capri in the 1st century AD and built a villa directly above. The ruins of Tiberius' **Villa Jovis** (Jupiter's Villa; open daily 9am–one hour before sunset) sprawl across an eastern promontory. Come for the fabulous view from the 297-m (974-ft) Salto di Tiberio (Tiberius' Leap), the last pleasure enjoyed by the emperor's enemies before being hurled over the edge.

Ischia

Lying at the western end of the Bay of Naples – reached by ferry or hydrofoil from Naples and Pozzuoli – the island of Ischia has won the overwhelming favour of German and Scandinavian tourists in the summer, thanks to thermal springs, fine sandy beaches, good facilities for watersports and naturism. Casamicciola Terme and Lacco Ameno are among the smarter spa resorts. One of the best beaches, pockmarked with volcanic steam spouts, is the **Lido dei Maronti** near the little fishing village of Sant'Angelo. Nature lovers can hike (or rent a donkey) up the extinct volcano of **Mount Epomeo**, at 788m (2,585ft), starting from Fontana; there are unforgettable views of the island and the Bay of Naples.

Pompeii

The everyday reality of Roman life comes alive in the bakeries, wine shops, groceries and brothels of **Pompeii**, a town of about 25,000 thought to have been founded in the 8th century BC. A cataclysmic eruption of Mt Vesuvius wiped out the flourishing town, along with neighbouring Herculaneum, on 24 August AD79, burying it under 7m (23ft) of ash. It remained entombed until 1594, when building work on an aqueduct led to its discovery, but excavation did not begin until the mid-18th century.

Pompeii street with a public drinking fountain

The road from the main gate (Porta Marina, the gate that led to the sea; open daily Apr–Oct 8.30am–7.30pm; Nov–Mar 8.30am–5pm; N.B. last entry is 1hr 30min hours before closure) passes on the right of the basilica, law courts and stock exchange to reach the **Forum**, the centre of town and its main public meeting place directly facing Mount Vesuvius. Imagine a vast square looking something like Venice's Piazza San Marco, with two-storey porticoes running along three sides and the six-columned **Temple to Jupiter** flanked by ceremonial arches at the north end. After earlier earthquake damage, the temple was used as the *Capitolium* and city treasury. You can see plinths from the square's statues of local and national celebrities and the white base of the orator's platform. In the northeast corner is the large, originally covered market *(macellum)*, while in the southwest corner is the **Basilica**, the largest building in Pompeii.

On the **Via dell'Abbondanza** running east from the Forum, ancient graffiti is daubed in red on the walls of the houses and shops. Election slogans, insults, obscene drawings – the tradition continued today has a long history. Prominent phallus signs often indicate a house of ill repute, with an arrow pointing upstairs to where the action was, although sometimes these were just a shopkeeper's good luck symbols. Notice the oil and wine jars in the shops, the bakers' ovens and flour-grinding mills shaped like

House and Garden

Unlike the predominantly aristocratic Herculaneum, ancient Pompeii's population of 25,000 was a mixture of patricians, nouveaux riches merchants, small shopkeepers, artisans, and slaves. They made their money from commerce in wool and wine. The typical patrician house had two storeys, with servants and lodgers living upstairs. The family's living and sleeping quarters surrounded a first courtyard or atrium. Opposite the entrance was a main living room *(tablinum)* backing onto the dining room *(triclinium)*. This looked onto another courtyard or Greek-style porticoed garden *(peristylium)*.

giant cotton-reels (excavators found a donkey lying by one he'd been turning when Vesuvius erupted).

Along at the **Stabian Baths** *(Thermae Stabianae)*, Pompeii's largest, you can see the men's and women's facilities – changing rooms, with clothes niches and three baths: cold, lukewarm and hot *(frigidarium, tepidarium* and *calidarium)*. The 2nd-century BC **Teatro Grande** seated 5,000

Temple of Apollo, Pompeii

spectators. Behind the stage was the Gladiators' Barracks, where 63 skeletons were found. Weapons and armour, along with Pompeii's more fragile works of art, are exhibited at Naples' Archaeological Museum.

Pompeii's Finest Villas

At the far end of Via dell'Abbondanza are two of the town's best villas: the **House of Loreius Tiburtinus** has a beautiful peristyle garden of fountains, water channels and cascades, one of them with paintings of *Narcissus* and *Pyramus and Thisbe*; and the **House of Julia Felix**, big enough to have been perhaps a luxury hotel, has its own bathhouse and a handsome portico of slender marble columns around the peristyle. Just to the south is the great **Amphitheatre** *(Anfiteatro)*, the oldest surviving in Italy dating back to 80BC, offering a fine view over the town from its upper tiers.

North of the Forum area are two of Pompeii's most important sites. The **House of the Vettii** (under restoration) was owned by two wealthy merchant brothers whose large home is one of the best preserved and elaborately decorated. Outside the main site to the north, the **Villa of Mysteries** *(Villa dei Misteri)* is Pompeii's other most cherished artistic treasure. The 'mysteries' are those depicted in a vast fresco of a young woman's initiation into the cult of Dionysius of Greek origin. Archaeologists, still unsure of what was involved, suggest that the gorgeously painted scenes of dancing satyrs, flagellation and a woman kneeling before a sacred phallus indicate rites that the town preferred to keep at a decorous distance. This splendid suburban villa was most likely the home of a priestess. The fresco's brilliant and little faded background of intense red to this day is still called 'Pompeiian red'.

In 2001 Pompeii was listed as a site in peril, prompting a master conservation plan. In practice, this means that only 25 of the 70 excavated villas are open at any one time.

Vesuvius (Vesuvio)

The old Roman name of Europe's most famous volcano means 'Unextinguished' – it is the only active volcano on the European mainland (there are others on the nearby islands of Sicily and Stromboli). **Vesuvius** rises to 1,281m (4,203ft), having gained 79m (259ft) in the big eruption of 1944 and subsequent smaller ones. Barring risks from 'unscheduled activity,' you can go as far as the 600 m- (1,960 ft-) wide steaming crater. Exploiting the fertile volcanic soil, some vineyards still produce the esteemed *Lacryma Christi* white wine. The **Eremo Observatory** halfway up the mountain has been studying eruptions since 1845 and has an impressive display of relief plans, seismographs and geological specimens spewed out of the volcano.

Aware that one million people are sitting on a time bomb and that a major eruption is a matter of when, and not if, in 2004 the Italian authorities offered each family 25,000 euros to move. However, the take-up has been minimal so far.

Herculaneum (Ercolano)

Some 7 km (4½ miles) from Vesuvius, **Herculaneum** is smaller and less renowned than Pompeii, but its compactness and better-preserved state give a more immediate sense of the shape and ambience of a whole Roman town. While Pompeii was incinerated by volcanic cinders, a lethal 20m (65ft) tide of ash and mud swamped

Herculaneum: smaller than Pompeii but better preserved

Herculaneum, hardening and covering the houses in a protective crust that kept upper storeys and even some of the woodwork intact. Rediscovered by well-diggers in the 18th century, the town is still being excavated, a delicate business as much of it is covered by the modern city of Ercolano. The **entrance** off the modern town's Corso Ercolano takes you around the archaeological site (open daily 8.30am–one hour before sunset) for a striking view down across the ancient town of terraced villas from which wealthy Roman landowners looked out to sea towards Ischia on the horizon. The three main streets dividing the town (Cardine III, IV and V) have kerbed pavements, lined with two-storey houses with balconies and overhanging roofs for shade. Most visited are the **Baths** *(Terme)*, which are in excellent condition, well equipped and practically laid out with separate areas for men and women.

At the southern end of Cardine V, the patrician **House of the Deer** *(Casa dei Cervi)* is named after its frescoes of two stags being attacked by hounds. In one of the rooms off the garden is a statue of a shockingly drunken Hercules, alleged founder of the ancient town. In the middle of Cardine IV, the **House of Charred**

The switchback Amalfi coast

Furniture *(Casa del Mobilio Carbonizzato)* has a uniquely preserved latticed divan bed and small table. Next door, the **House of Neptune** has lost its upstairs façade, but the ground floor wine shop with its narrow-necked amphoras on the shelves looks open for business. The inner courtyard has a lovely green-and-blue mosaic of Neptune with his wife Amphitrite.

The grandest of the villas, the **House of the Bicentenary** (excavated 200 years after the first 'dig' in 1738) stands on Avenue Decumanus Maximus on the northeast edge of town. It has splendid marble paving and, etched in the wall of one of the smaller rooms, a controversial cross regarded by some as one of the oldest Christian relics.

Sorrento and the Amalfi Coast

The coast curving along the southern arm of the Bay of Naples round the Sorrento Peninsula to Salerno is one of the most romantic and dramatic drives in Europe. The sinuous white-knuckle coastal road and its sheer drop of rugged cliffs and Falbero ravines can tame even the most audacious Italian driver. In former times, only brigands and pirates ventured out here, their ruined redoubts and look-out towers still dotting the hillsides and promontories. Now, road-side look-outs tempt travellers and aspiring photographers onto jutting crags high above terraces of orange and lemon groves, vineyards, walnut almond trees.

Surrounded on three sides by ravines above the sea, the pretty tree-shaded resort of **Sorrento** still retains something of its old-fashioned air and is a popular base for boat and car excursions along the coast and peninsula. Its local craftsmen are famous for their inlaid woodwork called *intarsia*. Compare their modern, sadly more commercialised wares with their forefathers' baroque furniture shown at the **Museo Correale** (open Mon and Wed–Sun 9am–2pm) in an 18th-century *palazzo* at the east end of town; the museum's porcelain collection is also worth a look.

Small, fashionable **Positano** spills down its hillside in a spectacular cascade of gleaming, bougainvillea-covered whitewashed houses dotted with gardens of oranges and lemons and terraces of colourful hand-painted tiles. The pebbly beach is lined with canvas umbrella-shaded chairs and fishing boats, and flanked by *pizzerias* and restaurants that stay open late into the night. In the little church of **Santa Maria Assunta**, with a characteristic majolica-tiled dome, see the 13th-century Byzantine-style altar painting. A wealthy international crowd keeps the four- and five-star hotels busy. With only two roads to speak of, most travel is by foot up and down its endless flights of steps.

The other lively resort, **Amalfi**, was once a powerful rival to the maritime republics of Pisa and Genoa, with trading posts in

Ravello teeters above the Amalfi coast

the 10th and 11th centuries in Palestine, Egypt, Cyprus, Byzantium and Tunis. Its two destinies come together in the **Piazza del Duomo**, where open-air cafés and ice-cream parlours look up a long monumental staircase to the Arab-Norman **Campanile** and polychrome mosaic façade of the Romanesque **Cathedral** (open daily 9am–8pm in summer, reduced hours in winter), built as a symbol of the republic's glory. It was begun in the 9th century, its massive bronze doors crafted in Constantinople and added to in the 11th century; the façade was added in the 13th, when the remains of St Andrew the Apostle were brought to its crypt from Constantinople. The ornate façade was rebuilt in the 19th century. The interlacing Arab-Norman arches of the 13th-century cloister, **Chiostro del Paradiso** (Cloister of Paradise), make a handsome setting for the summer recitals of chamber music.

Take a trip to nearby Conca dei Marini to view the stalactites of the **Grotta dello Smeraldo** (Emerald Grotto), where the waters are as brilliantly emerald green as those of Capri's Grotta Azzurra are blue.

Ravello

Set back on a high ridge 362m (1,184ft) above and behind Amalfi is the tiny and peaceful village of **Ravello**, once a hideout for Romans fleeing the Huns and Visigoths. Today it's a delightful resort of both modest and elegant hotels and villas, all stunningly situated. Directly off the main square, which is anchored by its imposing Romanesque **Cathedral**, built in 1076, is the **Villa Rufolo** (gardens open daily 9am–6pm, till 8pm in summer) with its mysterious polychrome arcaded arabesque cloister. Its hanging gardens of exotic flowers and palm trees and mesmerising views were the inspiration for Richard Wagner in 1880 for his last opera, *Parsifal*. They are the perfect location for outdoor classical concerts in summer. Reached by a rambling footpath is the 1904 **Villa Cimbrone** (open daily 9am–sunset). Its surrounding fragrant gardens also command a marvellous vertigo-inducing view of the craggy coastline and azure blue of the Gulf of Salerno. The view from here is the most photographed on the Amalfi coast.

Paestum

Italy has no more magnificent testimony of its many Greek colonies than this complex of wonderfully preserved Doric temples, a 40-minute drive south from Salerno, dating back to the 5th and 6th centuries BC. Standing alone in fields leading to the sea, their buff-stone columns take on a wonderful golden glow at sunset. Four temples loom over the forum and residential quarters. In pre-Roman times the town was known as Poseidonia, after the Greek god of the sea (whom the Romans knew as Neptune). After the town was abandoned to malaria and Arab invaders in the 9th century, the monuments disappeared under wild vegetation until their rediscovery 900 years later.

The Temple of Neptune, Paestum

The most spectacular temple, directly opposite the entrance to the site (open daily 9am–1hr before sunset), is the 5th-century BC **Temple of Neptune**. The roof has gone, but with its superb entablature and 14 fluted columns still standing, it is, together with Athens' Theseion, the best preserved of all Greek temples. To the south, the **Temple of Hera** (also known, mistakenly, as the Basilica) is a hundred years older and is Paestum's oldest, also predating Athens' Parthenon by one hundred years. The northernmost **Temple of Ceres** was built around 500BC, and was used as a church in the early Middle Ages, as attested by three Christian tombs.

Opposite the temples is an excellent museum (open daily 8.45am–7pm, closed 1st and 3rd Mon in each month), a treasure trove of Greek and Roman finds excavated from the site.

Puglia

Known to many under its Roman name of Apulia, this region stretches from the 'spur' of the Gargano peninsula to the heel of Italy's boot, endowed with a wild and unspoiled beauty over the gently undulating stony plateaux grazed by sheep and goats. Massive fortresses and fortress-like churches testify to the passage of the Normans and then the German emperors in the Middle Ages. In among the groves of olive, almond and fig trees, the stones have been gathered up from time immemorial to build the smaller, but equally sturdy, corbelled *trulli* (cone-shaped roofs) that crop up like so many mushroom clusters dotting the countryside. It is an exotically distant holiday destination popular with Italians and, increasingly, more adventurous Italophiles, both incredulous that this end-of-the-world piece of Italy is still part of Europe.

Gargano Peninsula

The peninsula's seaside resorts have good beaches among the pine groves, first-class camping and water-sports facilities, and are a base for excursions and walks in an attractive hinterland of rolling hills. The scenic coastal circuit begins in **Manfredonia**, with historical attractions such as the 12th-century church of **Santa Maria di Siponto** (southwest of town). **Pugnochiuso** is among the best of the beach resorts, along with **Vieste**, where Emperor Frederick II left a castle from which to view the Adriatic; the pretty fishing villages of Peschici and Vieste climb up the rocky promontory here.

Head inland through Vico to see the wild deer in the **Umbra Forest**. Perched on the Gargano heights south of the forest, **Monte Sant'Angelo** was a major medieval pilgrimage town, celebrated for its 5th-century sanctuary of **St Michael** (open daily 6.30am–7pm; earlier closure in winter) in a grotto where the archangel appeared to the Bishop of Siponto three times. The sanctuary inspired the building of the great French island-monastery of Mont-Saint-Michel after Bishop Aubert travelled to Gargano to collect a piece of St Michael's red cloak. From a Gothic portico in the middle of town, beside the massive 13th-century **Campanile**, a staircase of 90 steps takes you down to the sanctuary's 11th-century bronze doors. Notice to the left of the altar the beautifully carved stone episcopal throne.

From the north-coast resort of Rodi Garganico, you can take a 90-minute boat trip during the summer months out to the pine-forested **Tremiti Islands**.

Alberobello

This agricultural town is the centre of Puglia's famous *trulli*, the white-washed cone-shaped houses with russet or grey dry-stone roofs dotting the landscape like giant spinning tops turned upside down. The dazzlingly white cone is formed by small limestone slabs set in a spiral without mortar to bind them. Although the region's oldest surviving *trulli* date back only to the 16th century, the construction technique is believed by some to be prehistoric, brought here perhaps from Greece or the Middle East.

Trulli house at Alberobello

It is a joy to wander Alberobello's two neighbourhoods of *trulli* whose houses, shops and even churches – **Rioni Monti** and **Aia Piccola** – are protected as a *zona monumentale* (world heritage site). Shopkeepers are happy to let you climb up to their roof terraces for a striking view across a whole fairytale forest of some 1,000 *trulli* domes. Out in the country in and around lime-clad **Locorotondo** and **Selva di Fasano**, you'll find *trulli* (and *trulli*-inspired) farms, barns, grain silos and even petrol stations.

Northwest of Alberobello, a *strada panoramica* along a ridge overlooking the Adriatic coast leads to **Castellana Grotte** (open daily 8.30am–7pm) a spectacular cave system 60m (190ft) underground. Take a guided tour of the stalactites reaching down to fuse with stalagmites in glowing columns of red, green and pink.

Last but not least is Puglia's crowning glory, **Lecce**, dubbed the Florence of the South for its plethora of 16th- to18th-century *palazzos* of easily sculpted local limestone. Foremost is the **Basilica of the Holy Cross** (*Santa Croce*; open daily 8am–1pm and 4–7.30pm), the best example of the city's baroque heyday; and the **Piazza del Duomo**, ringed by the rebuilt cathedral and buildings of similar pedigree. The **Roman Amphitheatre** in the heart of Lecce dates from the 2nd century AD. It has a museum (open daily 10am–1pm) and also now serves as a concert venue.

Sicily (Sicilia)

The Mediterranean's largest island is in many fascinating ways a country to itself, seemingly not part of Italy or Europe at all, and if possible, it deserves a separate holiday to do it justice. However, for anyone who has a few days to spare for a first glimpse, we suggest some highlights: the capital Palermo, the ancient Greek settlements and the pretty coastal resort of Taormina.

Mondello, outside Palermo

Palermo

This bustling capital deserves the necessary effort to get into its colourful past. Cleverly integrating designs of Arab and Byzantine predecessors, the Norman palaces and churches join the crumbling grandeur of Spanish baroque façades in momentary triumph over the chaos of the modern port city. It is not always an easy city to love, but few leave unimpressed. The intersection of Via Vittorio Emanuele and Via Maqueda is the town's historic centre – **Quattro Canti** (Four Corners) – within a characteristic setting of two great baroque churches (San Giuseppe dei Teatini and Santa Caterina), the monumental 16th-century **Pretoria Fountain** by a Florentine sculptor and the *piazza* of the same name. The delightful Piazza Bellini includes the 12th-century church of **San Cataldo** (open Mon–Sat 9am–12.30pm) with its three little red domes and Arabic inscriptions. It was used for a spell in the 18th century as a post office, and has been restored to its bare Moorish beauty. Beside it, the Norman Gothic **La Martorana** (open Mon–Sat 8.30am–1pm and 3.30–6.30pm, Sun 8.30am–1pm) church, partly remodelled with a baroque façade and porch, has a fine campanile with four storeys of slender mullioned windows. Inside the porch, mint 12th-century **mosaics** show, to the right, Jesus crowning Sicily's Norman king, Roger I and to the left, his admiral, Georges of Antioch, at the feet of the Madonna. In the nave are glittering mosaics of Christ Pantocrator (Omnipotent Lord) with accompanying angels.

Arabic influence on Palermo church architecture

West along Via Vittorio Emanuele, the **Palace of the Normans** *(Palazzo dei Normanni)* was built by the Saracens as a 9th-century fortress and later turned into a royal residence, appropriate setting for the later brilliance and luxury of Emperor Frederick II's Sicilian court. Although it houses Sicily's regional government, tour buses line up for the jewel of the palace (and Palermo), one of Norman architecture's greatest achievements in Italy, the 12th-century **Palatine Chapel** (*Cappella Palatina*; open Mon–Fri 9am–noon and 3–5pm, Sat and Sun 9–11.45am). The noble Romanesque interior has a magnificent painted wooden ceiling with Arabic honeycomb motifs and stalactite pendentives. The **Byzantine mosaics** of the dome and apse depict Christ Pantocrator with the Evangelists, and Jesus blessing Peter and Paul; together with those of Ravenna, they are Italy's finest. The combination of figurative and intricate geometric designs was a collaborative effort of Syrian Muslim craftsmen with Byzantine Christians.

The pink-domed church of **San Giovanni degli Eremiti** (Via dei Benedettini; open Mon–Sat 9am–1pm and 3–7pm, Sun 9am–12.30pm) is an intriguing example of 12th-century Arab-Norman design. Its exotic character is enhanced by the twin-columned 13th-century **cloister** overgrown with tropical plants, orange, lemon and palm trees.

Housed in a 16th-century monastery, the **Archaeological Museum** (Via Bara all'Olivella, 24; open Mon–Fri 8.30am–1.45pm and 3–6.45pm, Sat and Sun 8.30am–1.45pm; hours may vary, so tel: 0919 611 6805 to check) displays superb statues and sculpted friezes from Sicily's various archaeological sites, highlighted by those from the Greek temples of Selinunte (600–500BC), which are on Sicily's southern coast.

Fresh fish at the market

Offset the historical with the theatrical, and make a visit to Palermo's daily **Vucciria Market** (entrance near Via Roma and Corso Vittorio Emanuele), an unmissable photo opportunity in what is the most famous of the city's daily markets. Vendors sing of their wares' quality in the local dialect, in a setting that feels more like North Africa than Europe. Sicily's major port city offers fresh seafood in a remarkable variety of shapes and sizes, and no-frills *trattorias* within or near the market promise an excellent, inexpensive lunch.

Monreale

The hilltop suburb of Monreale 8 km (5 miles) southwest of Palermo has Sicily's finest 12th-century **Cathedral** (open daily 8am–6pm; Treasury open daily 8am–noon and 3.30–6pm) and one of the best medieval mosaic cycles

Cathedral interior, Monreale

in Europe. Go round to the back of the church to see its wonderful russet and brown stone chancel of interlacing arches, Gothic rose windows and Arab windows with pointed arches.

In the grandiose interior, the luminous 12th- and 13th-century **mosaics** of the nave and apse depict the complete cycle of the Old Testament, replete with a 20-m (66-ft) Christ Pantocrator with saints, while aisle mosaics narrate New Testament miracles. The warm-hued human figures are thought to be the work of Venetian mosaicists.

The cathedral's beautiful **cloisters** (open Mon–Sat 9am–7pm, Sun 9am–1pm) offer a moment of spiritual meditation along the arcades of delicate carved twin chevron-fluted columns and an almost sensual pleasure among the exotic flowers and trees and Arab fountain of its garden. It is understandably a favourite spot for wedding photos.

Agrigento

Although known as the birthplace of the dramatist Luigi Pirandello (1867–1936), Agrigento's **Valley of the Temples** (*Valle dei Templi*; open daily 8.30am–1 hour before sunset) is its showpiece attraction, dating back to the 5th century BC. The **Temple of Juno**, with a sacrificial altar, stands in majestic isolation high on a ledge at the eastern end of the Via Sacra. But it is the **Temple of Concord** that is the best-preserved Doric temple in Sicily (if not the world), thanks to its subsequent use as a church in the 6th century AD. The golden glow of the Doric columns and the idyllic setting amid acacia and almond trees on a precipice overlooking the Mediterranean are enough to encourage you to worship a whole pantheon of Greek gods. Nearby is the oldest of the shrines, the **Temple of Hercules**, built in 500BC, whose eight 10-m (33-ft) columns have been re-erected to give some idea of its grandeur.

North of Temple Valley, next to the 13th-century Norman church of San Nicola, the small but important **Archaeological Museum** (open Sun and Mon 9am–1pm and Tues–Sat 9am–1pm and 2–7.30pm) has a fine marble statue of Ephebus (5th century BC); a gigantic telamon, a 25-ft sculpted male figure used to hold up a temple roof's entablature; and some fine Greek wine vessels.

Taormina

Sicily's most attractive resort town, already very popular in antiquity as a holiday spot for the Greek bourgeoisie from Syracuse, commands a splendid ridge-top view of the Mediterranean from its hillside villas and hotels. A popular port-of-call for countless cruise lines, the international crowds can be avoided for those lucky enough to be spending the night (a *funivia* cable car connects the hilltop town with Mazzarò beach below).

No Sicilian *passeggiata* is more celebrated than a promenade on the elegant pedestrian shopping street of **Corso Umberto** and out along the **Via Roma**, or through the subtropical vegetation of the terraced **Public Gardens**. With postcard panoramas south along the coast and to the volcano of Mount Etna to the west, the **Greek Theatre** (3rd century BC; open Mon–Sat 9am–

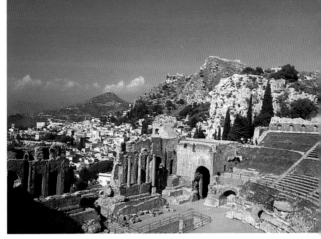

The Greek Theatre at Taormina

7pm, Sun 9am–1pm; winter till 4pm) is the only required site in town. It provides a unique setting for summertime festivals.

Excursions further up the mountain take you to two medieval fortresses, on foot to **Castello di Taormina** and, by car along a winding road, to **Castelmola** for grand views, although the summit of Etna is almost always swathed in clouds.

Syracuse (Siracusa)

This east-coast Corinthian settlement, founded in 734BC, was the most powerful of Magna Graecia's overseas colonies and, under Dionysius (405–367BC), a direct rival to Athens. In its heyday, its population was nearly treble the size of today's 118,000. It was here in the 3rd century BC that the famous mathematician Archimedes is said to have proven his water displacement theory in the bath, and then run naked into the street crying '*Eureka!*' (I've found it!). Today, the capital of Syracuse province is a cultured town of elegance and grace.

Syracuse's original settlement was the port island of Ortigia, joined by causeway to the mainland. Two pillars surviving from the Greek **Temple of Apollo** stand like a gateway, and the Spanish era has given it charming 17th-century baroque houses with iron balconies supported by floral carvings.

The graceful crescent-shaped **Piazza del Duomo**, surrounded by 17th- and 18th-century *palazzi* and the monumental façade of the cathedral, is the perfect place for breakfast. The church is an elaboration of the Greeks' Temple of Athena (5th century BC), its columns incorporated into the outside walls.

After many years of decay, the city is benefiting from restoration work. Much of Ortigia is under scaffolding, but this greatly needed work has brought a new confidence to the city.

Famous Greek Links

Syracuse's principal excavated site, **Zona Archeologica** *(Parco Archeologico della Neapolis*; open daily 9am–2 hours before sunset), is located on the northwest corner of the modern city. Rebuilt by the Romans to hold 15,000 spectators (one of the largest of the ancient world), the **Greek Theatre** dates back to the 5th century BC when Aeschylus himself arrived from his home at Gela to supervise productions of his tragedies. A classical drama festival is held here in May and June. The nearby **Paradise Quarry** *(Latomia del Paradiso)* provided the city's building materials and is now

Piazza del Duomo, Syracuse

a pleasant garden of oleander and orange trees. Its popular attraction is the cave that was dubbed **Orecchio di Dionisio** (Dionysius' Ear) by the painter Caravaggio in 1608 because of its acoustics.

Syracuse's history merits the world-class **Museo Archeologico Paolo Orsi** (open Tues–Sat 9am–2pm; Sun till 1pm), a crash course in understanding the Greek and other ancient cultures of the island.

Mount Etna

Europe's tallest volcano is still very active, as you'll see from the tell-tale yellow sulphur stains of mini-eruptions as you approach the crater, where the lava beneath your feet is still warm. The summit currently stands at 3,350m (10,990ft) above sea level, but varies according to eruptions' destruction or lava deposits. These deposits create fertile soil, in which vines and tomatoes flourish.

Etna continues to be extremely active (in 1998 serious eruptions lasted over eight months, while in October 2002 the volcano deposited large amounts of ash on the streets of Catania; there was also vigorous activity in 2003), and, at the time of writing, access to the craters was not allowed. To discuss options of getting close to the highly volatile volcano, usually by the northern route via Linguaglossa, contact the Alpine guides (tel: 095 647833) on the north side of Etna. For advice on current conditions and routes contact the Etna Regional Park (tel: 095 821111) in Nicolosi, or visit the information centres in Catania or Taormina.

Etna, Sicily's formidable volcano

WHAT TO DO

While you're wandering around the country's *palazzi*, churches, ruins and museums, you may wonder about everyday life for the average Italian. The concept of *la dolce vita* easily outlived its introduction in the early 1960s, given today's widening prosperity that has sustained the Italians' propensity for the sweet life. Their love of sport is contagious, elegant shops all too seductive, and the time-honoured theatricality extends from grand opera to colourful carnivals and religious processions.

SPORTS

Italian **football** (soccer) attracts a huge following, and in the major cities the teams are studded with top stars: in Turin (Juventus and Torino), Milan (AC and Inter), Rome (AS Roma and Lazio), and Naples (Napoli). For millions, Sundays are less sacred for morning Mass than afternoon football matches. On a day when Italy is involved in a major international football match, streets all over the country are deserted.

Cycling races are popular – especially the round-Italy *Giro d'Italia* in June. **Motor racing** fans can see the Italian Grand Prix at Monza, near Milan, or at Imola (the San Marino Grand Prix), near Bologna.

Bocce, the **bowling** game similar to French *pétanque*, is played in small towns wherever there's a shady patch of sand or gravel and a bar close at hand to serve a glass of wine or *grappa*.

On the beaches of the Adriatic coast, Italian Riviera, Sardinia, and Sicily, **swimming** is a pleasure that requires a few words of warning. Conditions of water pollution vary from year to year, but avoid a dip in the immediate vicinity of major industrialised port cities: Genoa, Naples and Palermo. Look out for red flags warning about dangerous undercurrents, and check to see that beaches are patrolled by lifeguards. At most seaside resorts like the Venice Lido or Sardinia's Costa Smeralda, expect to pay for umbrellas, deck chairs and the use of changing cabins.

For watersports at the resorts, you can often rent equipment on the spot for **snorkelling** and **wind-surfing** (particularly good on the lakes). **Scuba diving** is also popular. Some lake resorts also offer **water-skiing**.

Sailing is a popular sport around Sardinia and Sicily, and also on Tuscany's Argentario peninsula. Offshore **fishing** is popular all along the coasts, notably for tunny (tuna) off western Sicily, for swordfish on the east coast, and spear-fishing at Bordighera. For freshwater fishing in the inland lakes and rivers, you will need a permit from the local municipality.

Hiking is the simplest, most exhilarating way of seeing the countryside, whether in the Dolomites or the Alps, around the lakes and national parks, or trekking through the rolling hills of Tuscany or Umbria. Remember good shoes, light but solid, and some warm clothing. You can rent horses for **riding** throughout Italy – Tuscany and Umbria provide especially scenic terrain.

Golf enthusiasts can often play on local private courses with proof of their home club membership. Venice has an 18-hole course at the Lido's Alberoni. On the Riviera, try Rapallo, San Remo or Garlenda (near Alassio). Though a popular spectator sport, **tennis** is less widespread than in other major European countries, but it is growing in popularity. Your hotel can help you find a hard or clay court.

Heading for the Alps

Skiing facilities are first-class in many resorts in the Alps and Dolomites, and world championships take place at Cortina d'Ampezzo and Val Gardena. In adition to this the Winter Olympics 2006 are being held by Turin – the nearby resorts of Sestriere, Bardonecchia, San Sicario and others in the Via Lattea, the 'Milky Way Ski area, will host many of the events.

Inside Milan's La Scala opera

ENTERTAINMENT

When Italians moved the melodrama of their lives indoors, they called it **opera**. Most famous of the high temples of this art is, of course, Milan's La Scala (now newly restored), showcasing the works of Verdi, Bellini, Rossini, Puccini, and other Italian composers. The great stars and divas need a triumph here for true consecration. Its season is from December to mid-May. For good tickets you should plan well in advance through your travel agency, but your hotel may be able to help with seats made available by last-minute cancellations.

The other great opera houses are La Fenice in Venice, which finally rose from the ashes and re-opened in December 2003, Florence's Teatro Comunale, and the great Teatro San Carlo of Naples. But Bologna, Parma, Perugia, Rome, and Palermo also have fine regional houses. These show performances from December or January until late spring or early summer.

In the summer, the unparalleled venue for **open-air opera** is Verona's ancient Roman Arena, a unique location for perfor-

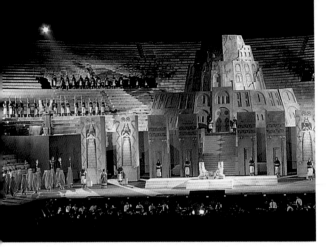

Verona arena

mances of Aida and other extravagant productions. In July and
August, Rome's Baths of Caracalla still offer the occasional per-
formance – though infrequently, due to the damage inflicted
over the years. Check with local tourist offices or newspapers
for a seasonal update. August's Puccini Festival in Tuscany's
Torre del Lago is held erratically according to funds available.
On the Adriatic, Pesaro honours its native son Rossini from mid-
August to late September.

Orchestral **concerts** of symphonic and chamber music, for
which it is usually easier to get tickets, are held in the opera houses outside and sometimes concurrently with the opera season.
Performances are also in Milan's Conservatorio and Rome's Accademia Filarmonica Romana or the Accademia Nazionale di
Santa Cecilia. Florence, Spoleto, Perugia, Ravenna, Rimini, Ravello, and Stresa all hold important music festivals. Tuscany, San
Gimignano and Lucca stage open-air concerts, while Amalfi's are
given in the cathedral cloisters. You'll never have to look long or
hard for music festivals in most towns. Lovers of Neapolitan **folk**

music can enjoy a whole week of it in early September at the Piedigrotta festival.

A great open-air festival of **jazz**, **pop** and **rock music**, the Estate Romana (Roman Summer), is held in the parks and gardens of Rome. Italy's most important jazz festival is held in Perugia in July, and there is another in Alassio in September. For information about Italy's music festivals (as well as theatre and film) refer to the website <www.italiafestival.it>.

One of the best ways to polish your Italian is at the cinema, where most foreign films are dubbed. International film festivals are held in several cities, the most important at Venice and Taormina.

For those who seek music action in discos and **nightclubs**, Milan seems to have the best selection. There are also many nightclubs attached to the hotels at the seaside resorts. Rome has plenty of nightlife – your best bet is to check the local listings or simply ask around.

Naturally enough, a visit to the **theatre** requires a good knowledge of Italian. You'll find the best productions in Rome and Milan, the latter famous for Giorgio Strehler's Piccolo Teatro, followed by those in Florence and Venice.

SHOPPING

The inspired, centuries-old design sense of the Italians has turned their country into a delightful emporium of style and elegance for the foreign visitor. The luxury goods of Milan, Venice, Rome and Florence – jewellery, clothes, accessories, especially shoes, but also luggage and household goods and items of interior design – are second to none in the world. Not inexpensive, but then the bargain here is not in the price, it's in the tradition of a centuries-old craft of meticulous workmanship.

There is an abundance of **gourmet delicacies** that make the perfect gift. Consider the cheeses, salamis, Parma ham, Milanese sweet *panettone* brioche, Ligurian olive oil; Siena's cakes and famous *panforte*, a spicy fruit-and-nut concoction;

and the small production Chianti and Orvieto wines that you may not find back home. If you've fallen in love with Italian coffee, why not buy a compact version of the *espresso* machine or packaged roasted beans? Italian kitchenware is in general beautifully styled with a great sense of colour and line.

In a country where civilisations have come and gone, there's a considerable traffic in **archaeological antiquities** but you can be fairly sure any ancient coins or artefacts are fakes. Many cities continue to be renowned for products of their **traditional crafts**: Naples' costumed hand-crafted figures for its nativity sets, Sorrento's *intarsia* (inlaid wood), Volterra's alabaster, Gubbio's ceramics, Florence's leather goods, Venice's glassware. For the rest, the widest range of Made-in-Italy products will be found in the large cities where tourism promises a brisk business.

Chic handbags and accessories

For quality goods, Italians prefer shopping in small boutiques. Family businesses often guarantee generations of good craftsmanship and personalised service. Mid-market **department stores** such as Standa and Upim are increasingly commonplace, while La Rinascente and Coin are the most upmarket. The former are useful for extra T-shirts or throwaway beach sandals, the latter for quality private-label fashion and accessories.

If you want friendly treatment in the more expensive stores, you're ahead of the game when dressed appropriately. Even the warmest-hearted sales assistant can

appear aloof towards cus-
tomers who are dressed poorly.
Credit cards work almost
everywhere but cash and travellers' cheques should be on
hand as a fall back. Haggling is
a thing of the past. You can get
an occasional small *sconto*
(discount) when buying in vol-
ume or paying in cash, but the
spread of foreign travel has
taught shopkeepers the going
international price for everything; except among antiques,

Fashion stores are everywhere

art and secondhand dealers, where negotiation is part of the business, you may get a cool response if you question (however po-
litely) the marked price.

Shopping in Rome

The capital's smartest and most expensive boutiques (even if
you're not buying, it's worth window-shopping for the superb
displays) are conveniently concentrated in a compact pedestrian
area around Via Condotti at the foot of the Spanish Steps. Here
you'll find the finest leather goods and of-the-moment fashions
from all the predictable high-priests (Valentino, Armani, Versace, Gucci, Missoni). Classic men's clothing shops such as
Cucci (with a C), Brioni and Battistoni are still going strong.

For sheer exclusivity in **jewellery**, there's nothing like the imposing marble facade of Bulgari (Via Condotti), the ultimate
monument to Roman luxury.

Two streets dominate the market in **art** and **antiques**, Via
Margutta and Via del Babuino and other off-shoots of the Piazza
di Spagna (as well as Via Giulia and Via Coronari).

On the outskirts of the chic shopping district around Piazza di
Spagna, you'll find mass-produced sweaters, jeans, and other
casual wear. More moderately priced leather goods can be found

Italy is known for its leather goods, particularly those in Florence

on the bustling Via Tritone, Via Nazionale and Via del Corso. For second-hand **bric-à-brac**, try shops around the Campo de'-Fiori and Piazza Navona. The Sunday morning flea market at Porta Portese in Trastevere is as much fun for the people watching as for the occasional bargains.

Shopping in Florence

If it has ceded to Milan its place as Italy's fashion capital, the old Renaissance city is still a centre of exquisite, if classic, elegance. The thoroughfares for the smarter **fashion boutiques**, for men and women, are Via de' Tornabuoni, Via della Vigna Nuova, and Piazza della Repubblica and Via de' Calzaiuoli.

Florentine **leather goods** remain unequalled. The country's, indeed Europe's, finest craftsmen once clustered in small leather workshops around San Lorenzo and Santa Croce, but goods now come mostly from factories in the periphery. The leather school tucked away behind the church of Santa Croce's sacristy (in what was once Franciscan monks' cells) is still going strong, allowing you a glimpse at the traditional making of leather goods such as handbags, wallets, gloves, belts and desk accessories.

The Ponte Vecchio is a picturesque place to shop for pricey but gorgeous gold and silver **jewellery**, designed with centuries of expertise. Less exclusive jewellery stores abound around town.

Inlaid wood or **semi-precious stones** *(intarsia)* is a venerated craft here, perfected in the 16th century. Furniture made in this way is likely to be expensive, but framed pictures of Tuscan landscapes or views of Florence are more moderately priced and, as souvenirs go, tastefully done. The town also specialises in bookbinding and beautiful stationery and paper products.

Antique shops are centred mainly around Borgo Ognissanti, Via della Vigna Nuova, Via delle Fosse, Borgo San Jacopo and Via Maggio. Even if you cannot afford the often prohibitive prices, they're worth visiting as veritable little museums of Renaissance and baroque sculpture and furniture. If the creative geniuses are long dead, master craftsmen continue the tradition of superb reproductions at negotiable prices.

Just 27 km (17 miles) from Florence, **The Mall** (Via Europa, 8, Leccio Reggello; tel: 055 865 7775; <www.outlet-firenze.com>) is one of Europe's most exclusive designer shopping outlets. Designer labels such as Armani Gucci, Valentino and Yves St Laurent can be snapped up at up to 80 percent reduction on the recommended retail price.

Venetian figurines

Shopping in Venice

One of the great adventures of shopping in Venice is separating the treasure-house from the tourist trap, distinguishing priceless gems from pricey junk. By and large, the better, more expensive shops are around Piazza San Marco. The shopping street of Mercerie has quality boutiques growing progressively moderate in price as they approach the Rialto from Piazza San Marco; so does the area west of Piazza San Marco. For cheaper purchases, head for the Strada Nuova leading behind the Ca' d'Oro towards the railway station.

The bargains or at least more authentic and tasteful products are to be found far from these main tourist centres, in artisans' workshops on the Giudecca, in the Dorsoduro behind the Zattere – to be hunted down or stumbled upon by chance.

Historical institutions that stand out among the **jewellery** and **glass** shops can be found in Piazza San Marco. For a cross-section of Venetian craftsmanship in more moderately priced **jewellery**, as well as **ceramics** and **glass mosaics**, take a look at Veneziartigiana, just off San Marco in Calle Larga, or in the artisanal shops on the Frezzeria. The famous

Glass and ceramic designs

Venetian **glassware** poses a problem of quality and price. Some of it is depressingly ugly, but there is also an admirable renewal in both classic and modern design. Just hunt carefully. Necklaces of crystal or coloured beads are popular for children, the antique glass beads collectables for adults. Prices in the Murano island factories are rarely better than 'downtown', but you do get a free demonstration and transportation thrown in. When choosing gifts to be shipped, remember to bypass the extremely fragile items and always ask for handling and insurance rates before you buy, as they can frequently double the price.

Visit Burano to see intricate **laceware** being made in the time-honoured manner in the island's small museum. The real thing is exquisite but exorbitantly priced, with many lesser-quality, machine-made pieces from the Orient being passed off as locally hand-made. Modern reproductions and interpretations of traditional patterns can be bought around Piazza San Marco.

Leather shoes are a speciality

The venerable craft of hand-made **paper goods**, **stationery** and **bookbinding** is easy to find. You can give your fancy-dress outfits a touch of Venetian class with the finely crafted papier-mâché **masks** made by workshops for Venice's Carnival.

The range of **fashion boutiques** around San Marco is small but select, with an emphasis on top-class shoes and other leather goods made in the Brenta area outside Venice.

Shopping in Milan

With the commercial leadership of the country, Milan is also the fashion capital. Names such as Armani, Prada, Versace, Dolce e Gabbana, Gianfranco Ferre and Moschino all began their careers in Milan. The designer district, around Via Montenapolone, is known as the Quadrilatero or 'Golden Triangle'. The area around Corso Vercelli and Corso Magenta has excellent shopping at more reasonable prices, as does the area around the Piazza Duomo and Corso Vittorio Emanuele II. Bargain-hunters looking for jeans, shoes and cheaper fashions should head for the popular stores along Via Torino and Via Manzoni. You'll find **art galleries** and **antiques shops** in the Brera neighbourhood and the side streets of Via Montenapolone (vias Borgospesso, della Spiga and Sant'Andrea).

Festivals

The Italians' attachment to regional customs and religious festivals has dwindled in the 20th century, but many continue for the tourist trade. Here is a far from exhaustive list of some of the main processions and festivities around the country.

January Piana degli Albanesi (near Palermo): a colourful Byzantine ritual for Epiphany.

February or **early March** Venice: historical Carnival, masked balls and processions in magnificent costumes. Viareggio: more contemporary Carnival with parade of floats. Agrigento: Almond Blossom Festival in Sicily.

April Rome: Pope's Easter Sunday blessing.

May Assisi: Calendimaggio Christian and pagan festival. Naples: Miracle of San Gennaro (liquefaction of the saint's blood, also on first Sunday in May, 19 September and 16 December). Camogli (Riviera): Fish Festival, communal fish-fry in giant pan. Gubbio: wooden candle race, crossbow competition. Orvieto: Pentecost feast of the Palombella (Holy Ghost). Florence: Maggio Musicale (May–June), musical performances in various venues throughout the city.

June Pisa: San Ranieri, jousting and torchlit regatta on Arno river. Florence: medieval soccer game in costume. Spoleto: Festival dei Due Mondi (June–July), international theatre, prose, music and dance performances by leading artists from Europe and the Americas.

July Siena: first Palio (2 July, *see page 106*). Sardinia: 'Sa Ardia' – more dangerous than Il Palio (6–7 July). Venice: Redentore regatta. Palermo: festival of patron Santa Rosalia. Rimini: Festival of the Sea. Rome: Noantri street festival in Trastevere. Perugia and other Umbrian cities: Umbria Jazz, one of the most important jazz festivals in Europe.

August Siena: Second Palio (16 August). Venice: Venice International Film Festival held at the Lido.

September Naples: Piedigrotta, Neapolitan music and cuisine and the 19 September feast day of San Gennaro. Venice: historical Regatta.

October Assisi: Feast of St. Francis. Perugia: Franciscan Mysteries.

December Rome: Christmas food and toy market on Piazza Navona. Assisi and Naples: nativity scenes in streets.

EATING OUT

The 'eating well' approach to life so treasured by the Italians is in abundance every mealtime in any town. From an early-morning coffee to an after-dinner *grappa*, eating and drinking here is always a memorable experience if not an art form.

WHERE TO EAT

For **breakfast** *(prima colazione)*, head for a *caffè* on the *piazza*, for an *espresso* or *cappuccino* with foaming hot milk (occasionally sprinkled with powdered chocolate), and a *cornetto* (sweet roll). Breakfast is often included in your hotel rate, but the more expensive the hotel, the less likely this is.

Ideal for those adopting a healthy 'sightseer's diet' of one main meal a day, preferably in the evening, with just a snack for **lunch**, informal bars known as *tavola calda* serve sandwiches and hot or cold dishes at the counter, with limited table space. More and more bars are offering simple, one-course, inexpensive lunches of salads or pastas. If you want to picnic in the park or out in the country, get your sandwiches made up for you at the *pizzicheria* delicatessen. Ask for a *panino ripieno* (a 'stuffed roll'), choosing from sliced meats and cheeses on display.

For **dinner**, it's useful to know that the more pricey restaurants *(ristorante)*, are often the worst value. In the more informal family-run *osteria*, *trattoria* (and *pizzeria*, which serves much more than just pizza), the relaxed and delightful ambience is extremely enjoyable, and the food often has more character. It's the custom to round off the bill with an extra tip in addition to

Pasta with clams

the service charge *(servizio incluso)*, something that the waiter does not often receive.

WHAT TO EAT

The classic cuisine of Tuscany and Bologna and the pizza and pasta dishes of the south are available everywhere, but try regional specialities as you travel around the country. The very essence of Italian cooking is its simplicity: fresh fish simply grilled; seafood served at room temperature as an hors d'œuvre, *antipasto*; thick, charcoal-grilled Florentine steak; seasonal vegetables without elaborate disguise, at most dressed with lemon, olive oil and pepper. Times are changing, but the following rule of thumb still applies: if it's not in season, it's not on the menu.

Many a *trattoria* sets out a table with an artistic display of platters of *antipasti*, where you're free to make up your own assortment *(antipasto misto)*. Both attractive and tasty are the *peperoni* – red, yellow and green peppers grilled, skinned and drizzled with olive oil, garlic and a little lemon juice. Mushrooms *(funghi)*, baby squash *(zucchini)*, aubergine *(melanzane)*, artichokes *(carciofi)* and sliced fennel *(finocchio)* are also served at room temperature. One of the most refreshing hors d'œuvres is the *insalata alla caprese*, slices of fresh mozzarella and tomato with sprigs of fresh basil, drizzled with olive oil.

Try tuna fish *(tonno)* with white beans and onions *(fagioli e cipolle)* and olive oil. Mixed seafood hors d'œuvres *(antipasto di mare)* may include scampi, prawns *(gamberi)*, mussels *(cozze)* sardines *(sarde)*, squid *(calamari)* and octopus *(polpo* or *polpetti)*.

Ham from Parma or San Daniele is served paper thin with melon *(prosciutto con melone)* or, even better, fresh figs *(con fichi)*. Most salami is tasty, though commercially produced, but look for the local products of Florence, Genoa, Naples, and Bologna.

> Cooking is essentially regional and terminology for food and dishes may vary. There are at least half a dozen names for octopus or squid.

Soups are the thick mixed vegetable *(minestrone)* or a

simple clear soup *(brodo)*. *Brodo* can have an egg beaten into it *(stracciatella)*.

Pasta

Italian restaurants traditionally serve **pasta** as an introductory course, *il primo*, not as the main dish. Even the friendliest restaurant owners will raise a sad eyebrow if you intend to make a whole meal out of a plate of spaghetti, whose portions, by the way, are not as hefty as those found outside the country.

It is said that there are almost as many different shapes of Italian pasta as there are days of the year – well over 300 at last count. Each sauce – tomato, cheese, cream, meat,

Salami by the kilo

or fish – usually calls for its own kind of pasta. Many restaurants usually offer one or two homemade pastas daily; the commercially processed pasta can be no less delicious.

Besides the classic spaghetti, the worldwide popularity of pasta has familiarised us with *tagliatelle* ribbon noodles (known in Rome as *fettucine*), baked lasagne with layers of pasta, meat sauce, and béchamel, and stuffed *ravioli*. From there, you launch into the lusty poetry of *tortellini* (reputed to be modelled on Venus's navel), *linguine*, flat *pappardelle*, short *penne* and ribbed *rigatoni*. Discover those types of pasta that are unique to the small towns you visit.

The **sauces** are no less abundant or savoury. Perhaps the most famous is *bolognese*, known in Bologna itself as *ragù*, made of minced beef, tomato purée and onions and never served with

Ravioli, one of many pasta dishes

spaghetti but with *tagliatelle*. Other popular sauces range from the simplest *aglio e olio* (garlic, olive oil and chilli peppers), *marinara* (tomato), *carbonara* (diced bacon and eggs), *matriciana* (bacon and tomato), Genoese *pesto* (fresh basil and garlic ground up in olive oil with pine nuts and parmesan cheese) and *vongole* (clams), to the succulent *lepre* (hare in red wine) and more unusual *al nero*, pasta blackened by squid ink.

For prince and peasant alike, Lombardy's Po Valley **rice** fields have made risotto a worthy rival to pasta, particularly in the north. The original version is cooked slowly in white wine, beef marrow, butter and saffron, and served with Parmesan cheese. Variations are endless: try those with mushrooms, chicken or seafood and seasonal vegetables.

Main Courses

For the main **meat** dish, veal *(vitello)* has pride of place among the meats. Try the pan-fried cutlet *(cotoletta)* Milanese-style in breadcrumbs, *scaloppine al limone* (veal fillets with lemon) or *vitello tonnato* (veal in tuna fish sauce). The popular *saltimbocca* (literally 'jump in the mouth') is a Roman veal-roll with ham, sage and Marsala wine, while *osso buco* is stewed veal shinbone. You'll find calf's liver *(fegato)* served in a Marsala wine sauce, *alla milanese* in breadcrumbs, or *alla veneziana*, thinly sliced and fried with onions in olive oil.

Beef *(manzo)*, pork *(maiale)* and lamb *(agnello)* are most often served simply charcoal-grilled or roasted *(al forno)*. In the south, meat is often cooked in a tomato and garlic sauce *(alla pizzaiola*). The most common chicken dishes are simply roasted (*pollo arrosto*), grilled or spiced with rosemary.

All the **fish** that you see displayed on ice are prepared very simply: grilled, steamed or fried. For a main course, look for *spigola* (sea bass), *triglia* (red mullet), *pesce spada* (swordfish) and *coda di rospo* (monk or angler fish). Be careful when ordering the *fritto misto*. Although this 'mixed fry' most often means from the sea, it can also be a mixture of breaded chicken breasts, calf's liver, veal and vegetables.

Aristocrats among the **vegetables** are truffles (*tartufi*) and big boletus mushrooms (*funghi porcini*), simply grilled. Try red peppers stewed with tomatoes (*peperonata*) or aubergine (*melanzane*) – sometimes stuffed with anchovies, olives and capers.

Desterts

Fresh peppers

Dessert means first and foremost *gelato*, the best ice cream in the world. But it's usually better (with wider varieties) in an ice-cream parlour (*gelateria*) than in the average *trattoria*. The coffee- or fruit-flavoured shaved ice, *granita*, is always refreshing.

When well prepared, *Zuppa inglese* ('English soup') should be an extremely thick 'soup' of fruit, cream, cake and Marsala wine. You may prefer the creamy coffee-and-masala *tiramisù* ('pick me up'). The *zabaglione* of whipped egg yolks, sugar and Marsala wine should be served warm.

Italy's **fruit** is always surprisingly sweet: grapes (*uva*),

peaches *(pesche)*, apricots *(albicocche)* and wonderful fresh figs *(fichi)*, both black and green. *Macedonia* is a fresh fruit salad. When berries are in season, don't miss them.

Of the **cheeses**, the famous parmesan *(parmigiano)* is eaten separately at the meal's end, not just grated over soup or pasta. Try the blue *gorgonzola*, *provolone*, creamy Piedmontese *fontina*, the pungent cow's milk *taleggio*, or ewe's milk *pecorino*. *Ricotta* can be sweetened with sugar and cinnamon as a dessert.

REGIONAL SPECIALITIES

Though most regional pastas and delicacies have spread nationwide, a few are still to be found principally in their place of origin.

Rome goes in for hearty meat dishes. Its *saltimbocca* vealrolls have gone around the world, but you mustn't wander too far from the Eternal City to get a real *stufatino* (beef stew) or *coda alla vaccinara* (braised oxtail with vegetables). Romans also claim the best roast kid *(capretto)* and spring lamb *(abbacchio)*. In the Jewish Ghetto try the *carciofi* prepared *alla giudea* or *alla romana* – whole baby artichokes, crisply deep-fried.

Tuscany produces excellent roast meats; *cacciagione* (game) is popular in season. *Pollo alla cacciatore*, 'hunter's style' chicken,

Ciabatta bread with mushrooms

has a tomato sauce embellished with mushrooms, shallots, herbs and ham. The classic charcoal-grilled T-bone *bistecca alla fiorentina* is often big enough to cover a plate and usually serves two people well. Adventurous palates enjoy the *trippe alla fiorentina*, tripe with tomato, marjoram and parmesan cheese. On the coast, look out for the *cacciucco*, a spicy fish stew of the sea's bounty in a slightly spicy tomato broth. *Baccalà* is dried salted cod.

Tuscans are known as 'bean eaters': try any variation of *fagioli*, white beans; they are a principal ingredient of the thick, wintery *ribollita* soup.

The cuisine of **Umbria** has great finesse. The roast suckling pig *(porchetta)* is especially fragrant with fennel and other herbs, and look for a succulent spit-roasted wild pigeon *(palombacce allo spiedo)*. Umbrians are proud of their *cacciotto* and *raviggiolo* ewe's

Summer fruit

cheese. In season, the truffle rules. The supreme pasta dish is served *ai tartufi neri* (with black truffles).

Milan has contributed its *risotto, cotoletta alla milanese* (breaded wiener-schnitzel style veal scallop), *osso buco*, and sweet *panettone* brioche to the nation. But it's kept for itself and its more robust visitors the *casoeula* – pork and sausages stewed in cabbage and other vegetables. Tough industrialists are weaned on *busecca alla milanese*, tripe with white beans. To fend off the autumn rains, the *polenta* cornflour served with so many savoury Lombard dishes becomes *polenta pasticciata*, a stout pie of mushrooms and white truffles in a béchamel sauce.

The choicest herbs in superb **Ligurian** pasta sauces is the basil of Genoa's *pesto*, best with the local *trenette* (large-size spaghetti). Rosemary is sprinkled on flat rounds of bread – *focaccia* – with olive oil. Wild aromatic greens are mixed with ricotta cheese in the ravioli-like *pansoti*, always served with a creamy walnut sauce. Liguria's fine olive oils rival those of Tuscany and Puglia. On *trattoria* menus, *misto di mare* is determined by the morning's catch from the fish-rich coastal waters.

Cooking in **Alto Adige** or South Tyrol is predominantly Austrian-style and is usually in German on the menu. Home-cured ham, *Speck*, is generally cut in paper-thin slices. In the mountains, try *Knödelsuppe*, a chicken or beef broth with simple dumplings. Austria meets Italy with *Spinatspätzle*, gnocchi-like spinach noodles with bacon and cream. *Friuli-Venezia Giulia* also continues the cuisine of the Austro-Hungarian empire – goulash and barley soup. Here, the great ham is *San Daniele*.

In **Venice**, the Adriatic specialities include cod, 'tenderised' for the great *baccalà mantecato* (cream of dried cod), and *grancevole* – beautiful red Adriatic spider crab. The humble combination of liver and onions, *fegato alla veneziana*, knows few rivals. Pasta appears less frequently than risotto, as popular here as in Lombardy, particularly with scampi or mussels, as well as the delightfully named *risi e bisi*, rice and green peas. An original creation of

Tomatoes are essential in many dishes

Harry's Bar, rendezvous of the international smart set, beef *carpaccio* is sliced raw and thin as Parma ham and served with an olive oil and mustard sauce. Delicious *cicchetti* are fresh, bite-size bar food (similar to Spanish *tapas*).

Bologna has an uncontested position of leadership in Italian gastronomy. Its specialities are the mainstays of the national cuisine, but are still best when enjoyed at home: *tortellini* pasta stuffed with different combinations of meat or cheese; *costolette alla bolognese* (breaded veal cutlets with ham and cheese); and the home-made *lasagne verde*, baked green pasta with beef *ragù* and béchamel sauce. The classic Bologna *mortadella* has little to do with the imitations found elsewhere. The star of neighbouring Parma is its *prosciutto* (air-cured ham) and parmesan cheese (labelled *parmigiano-reggiano*).

Turin is famous for its *bollita*, a most aristocratic boiled beef dish, with sausage, chicken, white beans, cabbage, potatoes and a tomato sauce. Not to be confused with the fondue from across the Swiss border, the *fonduta* of Piedmont is a hot dip of buttery *fontina* cheese, cream, pepper and white truffles (more delicate than black) that put this region on the culinary map. Its coffee houses filled with confections and locally made chocolate products are some of the nation's best.

The 20th anniversary of the Slow Food Movement is to be celebrated in 2006. The founding of this movement in Piedmont was to counter junk-food culture. The movement has been so popular that it now has more than 60,000 members over five continents.

In the South

In **Naples**, the tomato has been king since the Spaniards brought it from America in the 16th century. It's used in the simplest pasta, for which *alla napoletana* just means 'with a tomato sauce.' The classic pizza *(margherita)* uses local mozzarella cheese made of buffalo milk, with tomato sauce and basil or oregano. A handy version is the *calzone*, pocket-size pizzas filled with ham and mozzarella and folded in a half-moon. The seafood is excellent. Have morning coffee with a crisp Neapolitan *sfogliatella* croissant filled with sweet ricotta cheese. The *cannoli*, the south's unrivalled dessert, is stuffed with ricotta .

The lamb of **Puglia** is a royal dish. Try the *agnello allo squero*, spit-roasted on a fire of twigs perfumed with thyme and fine herbs; or *cutturidde*, baked with onion, parsley, tomatoes and sprinkled with *pecorino* cheese. *Gnemeridde* are chitterlings of baby lamb roasted or stewed with ham, cheese and herbs. Along the nation's longest coastline, try any of the great fish stews. Non-fish lovers can be happily satisfied with the region's unique *pasta orecchiette* ('little ears'), usually served with a sauce based on *cima di rape* – slightly bitter turnip greens.

The coastal resorts of **Sardinia** cook up a pungent fish soup *(cassola e pisci)* and roast eel *(anguidda arrustia)*.

Inland, kid *(capretto)* and suckling pig *(porceddù)* are roasted on the spit, as is the island's greatest delicacy, wild boar *(cinghiale)*. There's a great variety of country bread, the best being the charcoal-baked *civriaxiu*. Try it with the local *pecorino*, ewe's cheese.

Sicily has a rich culinary heritage based on both the sea and its inland agriculture. The *melanzana* (aubergine) is prepared in myriad ways, best perhaps simply grilled or in the popular *alla norma* sauce, with fresh tomatoes and mozzarella cheese. The legacy of the Arabs lives on in the abundance of citrus and almonds that appears in the island's justifiably famous desserts.

Fresh fish, Sardinia

WINES

Although the Italian wine spectrum includes far more than just **Chianti**, these are the most recognisable and are exported worldwide. The best Chianti Classico are produced in an historically designated area between Florence and Siena *(see page 101)* and distinguished by the *gallo nero* (black cockerel) label. Whereas most Italian wines can and should be drunk young, the Chianti Classico ages well. The best other Chianti reds are *Rufina*, *Montalbano* and *Brolio*, distinguished by a cherub on the neck labels.

Of the other Tuscan wines, the most appreciated reds are the refined *Vino Nobile di Montepulciano* and the powerful *Brunello di Montalcino*. The best of the Tuscan whites are *Montecarlo* and the famed *Vernaccia di San Gimignano*, both dry.

Orvieto in Umbria produces superb white wines, both dry and semi-dry. From the hilly area east of Rome come the refreshingly light *Frascati* and the famous *Est! Est! Est!* from Montefiascone on Lake Bolsena.

North of Tuscany's Chianti region, popular wine producers are centred around Verona and Lake Garda in the **Veneto** region, notably the velvety *Valpolicella*, light and fruity, and the light *Bardolino*. *Soave* is a dry white with a faint almond flavour. Try also *prosecco* – sparkling dry white wine which makes a wonderful *aperitivo*. The rosé *Chiaretto* comes from the region to the south of Lake Garda, and another rosé, *Pinot Grigio*, from Treviso.

Piedmont also has some of Italy's finest reds, particularly the powerful, full-bodied *Barolo*, and *Barbera* with a distinctive bouquet. The *Barbaresco* is the lightest of Piedmont reds. From south of Turin comes the champagne-like *Asti spumante*.

The *trulli* country of **Puglia** turns out some first-class white wines, notably *Locorotondo* and *Martina Franca*. Castel del Monte produces fine red, white and rosé wines. And if you like sweet wines, then try Trani's *Moscato*.

Among apéritifs commonly drunk, bitters such as *Campari* and *Punt e Mes* are refreshing with soda and lemon or orange; a glass of sparkling *prosecco,* a fraction of the price of champagne, is also popular. For after-dinner drinks, try the aniseed-flavoured *sambucca* with a *mosca* (literally a fly) coffee-bean swimming in it, or try Veneto's fiery *grappa*, distilled from grapes. An *amaro* (bitter) can be enjoyed before or after any meal.

Wine is the national drink

HANDY TRAVEL TIPS

An A–Z Summary of Practical Information

A

ACCOMMODATION *(alloggio)*
(See also CAMPING, YOUTH HOSTELS)

Every hotel, called *hotel* or *albergo*, is classified in categories by stars from one (basic) to five (luxury). Minimum prices in cities where most hotels are open all year are usually charged from November to April; in seaside or lakeside resorts, where many establishments are open only half the year, the low season is May–June and September in the north, April–June in the south. Breakfast is usually included but may be optional. During high season, many resort hotels require guests to stay a minimum of three nights on full-board *(pensione completa)* or half-board *(mezza pensione)*.

Pensioni. The term *pensione* encompasses everything from simple, family-style boarding houses to small elegant inns. These establishments are now considered hotels, and are rated by the star system. A *locanda* used to mean an inexpensive hostelry providing basic accommodation, nowadays it is often used to describe smaller 'boutique' hotels. Bed and breakfast is becoming increasingly popular in Italy, catering for all tastes from rooms in family homes to *palazzi*. For information contact Bed & Breakfast Italia, Palazzo Sforza Cesarini, Corso Vittorio Emanuele 11, 282, 00186 Rome; tel: (06) 6878 618; <www.bbitalia.it>. **Caffèlletto** offers bed and breakfast and apartments throughout the country. For information contact them at Via Procaccini 7, 20154 Milan; tel: 02 331 1814 or 02 331 1820; also visit <www.caffelletto.it>.

Motels in Italy are increasing in number and usually found along the *autostrada*. Some have a swimming pool, restaurant, and other facilities.

Religious institutions. Some monasteries and convents take in guests at reasonable rates. They provide comfortable rooms and often meals. For information, contact the regional tourist board.

Self-catering accommodation. Families staying for a week or longer in one city may find it more convenient and economical to rent a furnished apartment *(appartamento ammobiliato)* or villa.

If you have a car, you can also consider staying on a **farm**, in a simple cottage, a modernised farmhouse, or a 17th-century castle, and enjoy grape-harvesting, mushroom-gathering, fishing, horse riding or golf. For a variety of these options, from the affordable to the extravagant, contact <www.communicart.it>, <www.rentvillas.com>, <www.italianvillas.com> or Agriturist, the National Association for Rural Tourism (Corso Vittorio Emanuele II, 87, 00186 Rome; tel: (06) 6852 3337; <www.agriturismoinitalia.com>).

The Italian Alpine Club (CAI) owns several hundred **mountain huts**, and this organisation and the Italian Touring Club (TCI) publish books with detailed information. Write to: Club Alpino Italiano, Via E. Fonseca, Pimentel 7-20127 Milano, tel: 02 2614 1378; fax: 02 2614 1395, <www.cai.it>; Touring Club Italiano, Corso Italia 10, 20122 Milan; tel: (02) 85261/(02) 852 6320, <www.touringclub.it> or <www.cai.it>.

Do you have any vacancies?	**Avete camere libere?**
I'd like a single/double room	**Vorrei una camera singola/matromoniale**
…with bath/shower/private toilet	**…con bagno/doccia/ gabinetto privato**
What's the rate per night/week?	**Qual è il prezzo per una notte/una settimana?**

AIRPORTS (aeroporti)

Rome and Milan are Italy's principal gateway cities, but scheduled international flights also operate to Genoa, Naples, Turin, Venice, Pisa, Palermo and other major centres. The following website lists links for all of the Italian airports: <www.aeroporti.com>.

Rome is served by two international airports. Leonardo da Vinci (tel: 06-65951; <www.adr.it>) is known as *Fiumicino* and lies about 30 km (18 miles) southwest of the city centre. It is mainly used for scheduled flights. Fiumicino has two terminals, one for domestic and one for international traffic and a direct train every 30 minutes from 6.38am to 11.83pm that brings you to Stazione Termini, Rome's main rail station. The journey takes half an hour.

Ciampino (<www.adr.it>) is 15 km (10 miles) southeast of the city centre and mostly serves charter flights. There is a (fairly infrequent) bus connection to Anagnina, where you can pick up the underground train (Line A) to Stazione Termini. Also, the SM4 train runs to Termini station every 10–15 minutes.

Milan has two airports, Malpensa, 45 km (28 miles) northwest of the city centre, for international traffic, and Linate, about 7 km (4 miles) to the east, mainly for domestic and European flights.

From Malpensa there's a railway connection between Terminal 1 and Milan Cadorna station every 30 minutes between 5.30am and 1.30am, taking 45 minutes. There is also the Malpensa shuttle bus on the hour from Terminals 1 and 2 to Milano Centrale railway station, taking about one hour. From Linate, city bus No.73 operates every 10 minutes from the airport exit to central Milan and takes approximately 25 minutes. From international arrivals there is a STAM bus (tel: 02 717 106) every 30 minutes from 6.05am to 11.35pm which takes about 30 minutes. The website for both Linate and Malpensa is <www.sea-aeroportimilano.it>.

Taxi fares from airports to the respective city centres are approximately 10 times higher than the bus fares.

What time does the train/bus leave for the city centre?	**A che ora parte il treno/pullman per il centro?**

B

BICYCLE RENTAL (noleggio biciclette)

Cycling is a convenient way to get around the narrow streets of Italian cities. It is also an environmentally correct way to get around – especially on days when cars are prohibited from circulating. Ask your hotel concierge to advise when such days are enforced. For information on local rental agencies and organised bike tours, contact the local regional tourist board.

C

CAMPING (*campeggio*)

There are more than 2,000 official campsites in Italy. Addresses and full details of amenities are given in the directory *Campeggi in Italia*, published annually by the Italian Touring Club (TCI; <www.touringclub.it>) and sold in Italian bookstores. A free list of sites, with location map, published by Federcampeggio (*Federazione Italiana del Campeggio e del Caravanning*), is available from the Italian National Tourist Office (*see page 250*) or from Federcampeggio (Via Vittorio Emanuele 11, P.O. Box 23, 50041 Calenzano, Florence, tel: 055-882 391, fax: 055-882 5918).

The *Camping Card International*, a pass that entitles holders to modest discounts and insurance coverage throughout Europe, is required at many campsites in Italy. It can be obtained through your camping or automobile association or through the TCI or *Federcampeggio*.

It is inadvisable to camp outside official sites. If you do so, choose sites where there are other campers, and obtain the permission from the owner of the property or ask at the local police station or tourist office.

Is there a campsite near here?	**C'è un campeggio qui vicino?**
Have you room for a tent/ caravan?	**C'è posto per una tenda/ roulotte?**
May we camp here?	**Possiamo campeggiare qui?**

CAR RENTAL (See also DRIVING)

The major international car rental companies have agency windows in the arrival area of Italy's airports and are listed in the yellow pages of the telephone directory under 'Autonoleggio.'

I'd like to rent a car.	**Vorrei noleggiare una macchina.**
...for one day/a week	**...per un giorno/una settimana**
I want full insurance.	**Voglio l'assicurazione completa.**

The best rates are usually found by booking directly with an international rental company and paying before you leave home, or as part of a 'fly-drive' deal. Check that the quoted rate includes Collision Damage Waiver, unlimited mileage and tax, as these can greatly increase the cost. You must be over 21 to rent a car, and you will need to have held a full, valid driver's licence for at least 12 months, which should be shown at the time of pick-up. You must also show your passport and a major credit card, as cash deposits are prohibitively large.

Petrol *(benzina)* is priced per litre (4 litres to a gallon). NB Some petrol stations in Italy, mostly in the south, do not accept credit cards.

CLIMATE *(clima)*

The average daily temperatures for Milan and Rome are as follows:

			J	F	M	A	M	J	J	A	S	O	N	D
Milan	max.	°C	5	8	13	18	23	27	29	28	24	17	10	6
	min.	°C	0	2	6	10	14	17	26	19	16	11	6	2
Rome	max.	°C	11	13	15	19	23	28	30	30	26	22	16	13
	min.	°C	5	5	7	10	13	17	20	20	17	13	9	6
Milan	max.	°F	40	46	56	65	74	80	84	82	75	63	51	43
	min.	°F	32	35	43	49	57	63	67	66	61	52	43	35
Rome	max.	°F	52	55	59	66	74	82	87	86	79	71	61	55
	min.	°F	40	42	45	50	55	63	67	67	62	55	48	44

In the Alpine region, winters are long and cold, but often sunny, while summers are short and pleasantly cool. The northern lakes and Po Valley see cold and foggy winters and warm, sunny summers. The rest of the country, even the northern Ligurian coast, has mild weather in winter. Summers are dry and hot to scorching, depending on how far south you go, but sea breezes often compensate for the torrid heat.

The best time for a visit to the Ligurian and Adriatic coasts is from May/June to September. Before or after this period it can be rather chilly and rainy with most hotels closed and beaches practically deserted. The best time to visit the cities of Italy is in spring or autumn – between April and June and again in September and October – when the weather is most pleasant. However, the streets can be just as crowded. To check the weather on the web, try: <www.wunderground.com> and <www.met-office.gov.uk>, both with five-day forecasts for Italian cities.

CLOTHING (*vestiti*)

If you're travelling in northern Italy in winter, you'll need boots and an overcoat, but in the south a lightweight coat will be adequate. During early spring and late autumn, you should bring light to medium-weight clothing and rainwear for those brief but regular showers. Summer evenings can be cool, so pack a jacket or wrap. All year round, comfortable walking shoes are indispensable. Remember that Italy's churches are places of worship as well as works of art and architecture, and you should dress respectably if you intend to visit them – shorts, miniskirts and bare shoulders are frowned upon and may even mean that you are not allowed entry.

COMPLAINTS (*reclamo*)

Complaints should first be made to the management (*direttore*) of the establishment concerned. If satisfaction is not obtained, threaten to make a formal declaration (*faccio la denuncia alla questura*) although carrying this out will be time-consuming. To avoid problems, always establish a price in advance with all parties involved, such as porters at stations. For taxi fare complaints, refer to a notice, in four languages, which is affixed by law in each taxi, specifying extra charges (airport runs, baggage surcharge, Sunday or holiday rates, night surcharge etc) in excess of the meter rate.

CRIME AND SAFETY (*criminalità e sicurezza*)

Cases of violence against tourists are rare, but petty theft is an endless annoyance, and tourists are always easy targets for robbery. Check whether your home insurance policy covers theft or loss of personal effects while abroad; if it does not, it is advisable to take out separate insurance.

Take usual precautions against theft – don't carry large amounts of cash; leave your valuables in the hotel safe, not in your room; never leave your bags or valuables in a parked car, whether in view or in the boot. The main danger is generally from pickpockets, especially around tourist attractions, busy markets and on buses. Beware of gypsy girls with babies or young children – while they distract your attention begging for coins, an accomplice may be behind you dipping into pockets and bags. If you have a shoulder bag, wear it across your body – it's harder to snatch. Make photocopies of your tickets, driver's licence, passport and other vital documents to facilitate reporting a theft and obtaining replacements.

I want to report a theft.	**Voglio denunciare un furto.**
My wallet/passport/ticket has been stolen.	**Mi hanno rubato il portafoglio/ il passaporto/il biglietto.**

Any theft or loss must be reported immediately to the police. Obtain a copy of the report in order to comply with your travel insurance. If you lose your passport, you must also inform your consulate or embassy (*see page 234*).

CUSTOMS (*dogana*) AND ENTRY REQUIREMENTS

For citizens of EU countries, a valid passport or identity card is all that is needed to enter Italy for stays of up to 90 days. Citizens of Australia, New Zealand and the US also require only a valid passport.

Visas (*permesso di soggiorno*). For stays of more than 90 days a visa or residence permit is required. Regulations change from time to time, so check with the Italian Embassy in your home country before travelling.

Free exchange of non-duty-free goods for personal use is allowed between EU countries. Refer to your home country's regulating organisation for a current complete list of import restrictions.

Currency restrictions. Tourists may bring an unlimited amount of Italian or foreign currency into the country. On departure you must declare any currency beyond the equivalent of €10,300, so it's wise to declare sums exceeding this amount when you arrive.

I've nothing to declare.	**Non ho niente da dichiarare.**
It's for my personal use.	**È per mio uso personale.**

D

DRIVING

Motorists bringing their vehicle into Italy need a full driver's licence (an International Licence unless you are from another EU country), an International Motor Insurance Certificate, and a Vehicle Registration Document. Drivers entering Italy in a private car registered to another person must have the owner's written permission, translated. A green insurance card is not a legal requirement, but it is strongly recommended for travel within Italy. Foreign visitors must display an official nationality sticker, and, if you are coming from the UK, Ireland or Malta, headlights must be adjusted for driving on the right.

The use of seat belts in front and back seats is obligatory; fines for non-compliance are stiff. It is now also mandatory to switch on car headlights during the daytime. A red warning triangle must be carried in case of breakdown. Motorcycle riders must wear helmets. The ACI (Automobile Club d'Italia; <www.aci.it>) gives on-line information worth consulting before your departure. The head office is in Via Mansala, 8, 00185 Rome, tel: (06) 49981, fax: (06) 4998 2469.

Driving conditions. Drive on the right, overtake on the left. Give way to traffic coming from the right. Speed limits: 50 km/h (30 mph) in town, 90 km/h (55 mph) on dual carriageways, and 130 km/h (80 mph) on motorways.

Dual carriageways *(superstrade)* and most motorways *(autostrade)* are skilfully designed for fast driving. Italian *autostrade* are toll roads – you take an entry ticket from an automatic machine when you enter the motorway, and pay at the other end for the distance travelled. Do not to enter exclusive 'TelePass' (automatic toll meter) lanes, otherwise you will be forced to reverse and incur a fine.

On country and two-lane roads you'll encounter bicycles, scooters, three-wheeled vehicles and the occasional horse-drawn cart. These rarely have lights, and are a danger after dark.

Rules and Regulations. Italian traffic police *(polizia stradale)* are authorised to impose on-the-spot fines for speeding and other traffic offences, such as driving while intoxicated or stopping in a no-stopping zone. All cities and many towns and villages have signs posted at the outskirts indicating the telephone number of the local traffic police headquarters or *Carabinieri* (see POLICE). Police have recently become strict about speeding, a national pastime, and are beginning to install hidden speed regulators with cameras. They also frown on the widespread practice of 'jumping the light.'

Fuel. Petrol *(benzina)* is sold in three grades: Senza Piombo (unleaded; 95 octane), Super Unleaded (98 octane), and Super (leaded, 98 octane), as well as diesel fuel *(gasolio)*. Petrol stations on motorways are generally open 24-hours; be warned that others usually close for lunch, opening from 7am–12.30pm and 3pm–7.30pm, and are often closed on Sundays and holidays. Many offer self-service by an automatic payment machine which accepts notes and sometimes credit cards. In the south, cash is still the preferred form of payment.

Parking (*posteggio/parcheggio*). A blue-and-white sign with a 'P' indicates legal parking places. If there is a bicycle or scooter image on the sign, it is not meant for car parking. In cities, the wisest course is to find a supervised car park (*parcheggio custodito*) near your hotel and leave your car there for the duration

Curva pericolosa	Dangerous bend/curve
Deviazione	Detour
Divieto di sorpasso	No overtaking
Divieto di sosta	No stopping
Lavori in corso	Road works/Men working
Pericolo	Danger
Rallentare	Slow down
Senso vietato/unico	No entry/One-way street
Vietato l'ingresso	No entry
Zona pedonale	Pedestrian zone
ztl	Limited traffic zone
driving licence	**patente**
car registration papers	**libretto di circolazione**
Green Card	**carta verde**
Can I park here?	**Posso parcheggiare qui?**
Are we on the right road for …?	**Siamo sulla strada giusta per …?**
Fill the tank please.	**Per favore, faccia il pieno de …**
super/normal	**super/normale**
lead-free/diesel	**senza piombo/gasolio**
I've had a breakdown.	**Ho avuto un guasto.**
There's been an accident.	**C'è stato un incidente.**

of your stay. Be sure to check the opening hours as few are accessible 24 hours a day. There are authorised parking areas *(parcheggio a pagamento)*, often near the main railway station, where you pay by the hour, as well as car parks outside the centre with bus connections into town. Many larger towns have multi-storey car parks *(autorimessa or garage)*. In a 'Zona Disco' you need a parking disc *(disco di sosta)*, obtainable from petrol stations. Set it to show the time you arrived and it will indicate when you have to leave. Then display it in the car, visible through the windscreen. Don't leave your car in places marked by yellow-and-black stripes, or where it says 'Zona Rimozione' (removal zone), 'Zona Verde' (green zone), 'Zona Pedonale' (pedestrian zone), or in a 'Sosta Vietata' (no parking) or 'Divieto di Sosta' (no stopping) zone; if you park there, your car will likely be towed away.

Never leave valuables or leave the glove compartment open.

If You Need Help. Should you be involved in a road accident, dial the all-purpose emergency number 113, or 112 for the *Carabinieri*. Every 2 km (1½ miles) on the motorway there's an emergency call box marked 'SOS'. If you require a recovery vehicle, call 116 for assistance, but be aware that you will be charged; be sure that you have breakdown insurance coverage before you leave home. If your car is stolen or broken into, contact the Urban Police Headquarters *(Questura)* and get a copy of their report for your insurance claim.

Road signs. Most road signs in Italy are international. Here are some written signs you might also come across:

E

ELECTRICITY

220V/50Hz AC is standard. An adaptor for continental-style sockets is needed; American 110V appliances require a transformer.

EMBASSIES AND CONSULATES *(ambasciate; consolati)*

Contact your embassy or consulate when in trouble (loss of passport, problems with the police, serious accidents). All embassies are in Rome, but many countries also maintain consulates in other Italian cities.

Australia Via Alessandria, 215, tel: 06 852721, fax: 06 8527 2300, <www.australian-embassy.it>.

Canada Via G. Battista de Rossi 27, tel: 06 445981, fax: 06 4459 8750, <www.canada.it>.

New Zealand Via Zara 28, tel: 06 441 7171, fax: 06 440 2984, <www.nzembassy.com>.

Republic of Ireland Piazza Campitelli, 3, tel: 06 697 9121.

South Africa Via Tanaro 14, tel: 06 8525 4100, fax: 06 8525 4300, <www.sudafrica.it>.

UK Via XX Settembre 80a, tel: 06 4220 2334, fax: 06 487 3324, <www.britain.it>.

US Via Vittorio Veneto 119/A–121, tel: 06 46741, fax: 06 488 2672/4674 2356, <www.usis.it/>.

EMERGENCIES

If you don't speak Italian, find a local to help you, or talk to the English-speaking operator on the assisted service, tel: 170.

Police	112
General Emergency	113
Fire	115
Paramedics	118

Please can you place an emergency call to the …?	**Per favore, può fare una telefonata d'emergenza …?**
police	**alla polizia**
fire brigade	**ai vigili del fuoco**
hospital	**all'ospedale**

G

GAY AND LESBIAN TRAVELLERS

ARCI-gay, the national gay rights organisation, is a great source for finding bars, hotels, beaches and other gay-friendly localities. More than 15 cities have an ARCI-gay office. Contact Arcigay-Milano; Via Evangelista Torricelli, 19, 20136 Milano, tel: 02 5810 0399, help line 02 8940 1749, fax: 02 8394 604. A reference magazine widely available in Italy is *Spartacus International Gay Guide*.

GETTING TO ITALY

By Air

Scheduled flights. Rome's Leonardo da Vinci (Fiumicino) and Milan's Linate and Malpensa airports (*see page 224)* are the main gateways to Italy, though certain international flights operate into Bologna, Florence, Genoa, Naples, Pisa, Turin, Venice, Sardinia and Sicily. From Milan and Rome there are regular scheduled flights to some 30 destinations within Italy. The most economical flights within Europe are operated by easyJet, Ryanair and British Midland, all of which fly to Italian cities from points across Europe.

Package tours are offered by a wide range of tour operators and travel agents. Many package tours start out in Rome and include a choice of guided tours throughout the country. If you book a charter fare and plan to tour Italy independently, look into fly-drive with flight and car rental included. The Italian National Tourist Office distributes lists of tour operators offering tours and special-interest holidays, including language, art, and architecture courses.

By Road (See also DRIVING)

The road system within Italy is very manageable from north to south including ferry transport connections to Sicily and Sardinia. It is accessible through France, Switzerland and Austria. Contact your local automobile club to map out the best route.

By Rail

Ferrovie dello Stato (FS), Italian State Railways, tel: 051 257911 or 848 888088 (toll-free in Italy), <www.fs-on-line.com>. They will help plan an itinerary. Offices abroad include:

Australia, Cit, 263 Clarence Street, Sydney, tel: 612 9267 1255.

Canada Cit World Travel Group, 1450 City Councillors, Suite 750, Montreal Que. H3A IV4, tel: 541 846 431 0800; Alba Tours Canada Leisure Group, 130 Merton Street, Toronto, Ont. M5R 3J8, tel: 416 746 2890.

South Africa World Travel Agency, 8th Floor, Everite House 20, De Korte Street Braamfontein, Johannesburg.

UK Rail Choice Delta House, 175–177 Borough High Street, London SE1 1XP, tel: 020 7939 9915, fax: 020 7939 9916. For information on rail journeys to Italy, including Eurostar, contact the Rail Europe Travel Centre, tel: 0870 848848; <www.raileurope.co.uk>.

US 500 North Michigan Avenue, Suite 1310, Chicago, IL 60611, tel: 312 644 0990; 6033 West Century Boulevard, Suite 1090, Los Angeles, CA 90045, tel: 213 215 9814, 342 Madison Avenue, Suite 207, New York, NY 10173, tel: 212 697 1482 or 800 248 7245.

Travellers from countries where the FS is not represented should contact their national railways or a travel agency. For information also tel: Trenitalia on 011 892 021 or visit <www.trenitalia.com>.

You can plan as you go with human and computerised information points, where you can get train times and fares from a touchscreen terminal. Train travel is fairly cheap. Ticket machines take credit cards as well as cash.

European national railways offer a wide range of bargain tickets. Many of the rail passes mentioned below must be obtained before leaving home. The *Eurailpass,* an individual ticket available to people residing outside Europe, is valid for unlimited rail travel in 17 European countries (Austria, Belgium, Denmark, Eire, Finland, France, Germany, Greece, Hungary, Italy, Luxembourg, the Netherlands, Norway, Portugal, Spain, Sweden and Switzerland), including travel on some private railways, buses, and many ferry boats and steamers (website: <www.eurail.com>; also available from travel agencies). The *Eurail Saverpass* is a first-class ticket for two or more people travelling together, while the *Eurail Flexipass* offers more flexibility for 10 days' travel within a two-month period. The *Eurail Youthpass* for those under 26 allows one or two months of unlimited second-class rail travel. Surcharges are sometimes imposed on fast trains such as EuroCity (EC), Intercity (IC), Rapido (R) and TGV, and for certain ferry crossings during high season.

For residents of European countries, there's the *Carta Argento*, which entitles senior citizens to purchase train tickets at reduced prices. A family of three to five people can buy a *L'Offerta Famiglia* card giving a 30 percent reduction for all national and EuroCity trains. Europeans under 26 years of age can purchase an *Inter-Rail* zone card, good for up to two months of unlimited second-class travel.

The *Biglietto Chilometrico* is valid for two months of first- or second-class travel. It can be used by as many as five people, even if not related, for 20 trips totalling a maximum of 3,000 km (1,864 miles), with supplements for Rapido, Intercity, and Eurostar trains. For senior citizens a *Rail Europe Senior Card* is available for one year – visit <www.senior-railcard.co.uk>.

Although less frequent these days, be aware of the infamous Italian *sciopero* (train strike) that can last from a few hours to a few days. Check with your hotel before going to the station as they are always publicised in advance.

When's the next bus/ train to …?	**Quando parte il prossimo autobus/treno per …?**
single (one-way)	**andata**
return (round-trip)	**andata e ritorno**
first/second class	**prima/seconda classe**
What's the fare to …?	**Qual è la tariffa per …?**

GUIDES AND TOURS

Local tourist offices and major hotels can help you find qualified guides and give you a list of tours. Private tour guides give you access to lesser-known sights and shopping and it is best to book in advance from home during high season. Contact your travel agent or look up 'tour guides Italy' on your favourite on-line search engine.

Can you recommend a sightseeing tour/an excursion? We'd like an English-speaking guide.	**Può consigliare un giro turistico/una gita? Desideriamo una guida che parla inglese.**

H

HEALTH AND MEDICAL CARE

If your health-insurance policy does not cover you while abroad, take out a short-term policy with your insurance company, automobile association, or travel agency before leaving home. EU citizens are entitled to free emergency hospital treatment if they have a European Health Insurance card. You may have to pay part of the price of treatment or medicine. If so, keep receipts so that you can claim a refund when you return home.

If you need medical care, ask your hotel concierge or contact your local consulate or embassy to find a doctor (or dentist) who speaks English. Throughout Italy, in an emergency you can telephone 113 (the national police) for an ambulance.

Tap water is safe to drink unless there is a sign reading 'Acqua Non Potabile.'

HOLIDAYS

Banks, government offices, most shops, and some museums and galleries are closed on the following days:

1 January	*Capodanno/Primo dell' Anno*	New Year's Day
6 January	*Epifania (La Befana)*	Epiphany
25 April	*Festa della Liberazione*	Liberation Day
1 May	*Festa del Lavoro*	Labour Day
15 August	*Ferragosto*	Assumption
1 November	*Ognissanti*	All Saints' Day
8 December	*L'Immacolata Concezione (Forte dell 'Immacolata)*	Immaculate Conception
25 December	*Natale*	Christmas Day
26 December	*Santo Stefano*	St. Stephen's Day
Moveable date:	*Pasqua*	Easter
	Lunedì di Pasqua	Easter Monday

Shops and offices may also close on local feast days held in honour of a town's patron saint.

L

LANGUAGE

Despite the many different dialects around the country, standard Italian is understood by everyone in Italy. University students and staff at the major hotels and shops in the big cities and resort areas will usually speak some English, so you can easily get by without a word of Italian. However, it is polite to learn at least a few basic phrases. Local people will welcome and encourage any attempt you make.

The Berlitz phrase book *Italian For Travellers* covers most of the situations you're likely to encounter during your travels in Italy. Also useful is the Berlitz Italian-English/English-Italian Pocket Dictionary, which contains the basic vocabulary you will need, plus a menu-reader supplement.

LAUNDRY AND DRY CLEANING *(lavanderia, tintoria)*

There are coin-operated, self-service launderettes in all of the major cities; ask your concierge where the closest one is located. Next-day full service is provided by a *tintoria* or *lavanderia*. Specify if you would like your items washed and ironed *(lavata e stirata)* or dry-cleaned *(lava a secca)*. All of these solutions are more economical than the in-house service offered by hotels. If you are scheduled to leave town, bear in mind that service is not always as speedy as it is at home.

M

MAPS

Tourist offices give away basic street plans featuring a selection of local information. More detailed maps are on sale at newsstands.

I'd like a street plan of…	**Vorrei una pianta della città…**
a road map of this region.	**una carta stradale di questa regione.**

MEDIA

Newspapers and magazines *(giornale, rivista)*. You can find newspapers in English at airports and in most city-centre news-stands *(edicola)*. *The Wall Street Journal Europe* and *The International Herald Tribune* are available on the day of publication, as well as UK broadsheets, including *The Times, Guardian, Telegraph,* and some tabloids.

Radio and TV *(radio, televisione)*. The Italian state TV network, the RAI *(Radio Televisione Italiana)*, broadcasts three TV channels, which compete with six independent channels. All programmes are in Italian, including British and American feature films and imports, which are dubbed. CNN (in English) is transmitted on TMC in the morning from 4.20am–6am, and from 3.15am on Sundays. Most hotels and rental properties have cable connections which show CNN Europe, CNBC, and other channels that offer world news in English including BBC World and Sky. The airwaves are crammed with radio stations, most of them broadcasting popular music. The BBC World Service can be picked up on 1209.5 AM in the morning and 733 AM in the evenings.

MONEY

Currency *(soldi)*. In common with most other European countries, the official currency used in Italy is the euro (€). Notes are denominated in 5, 10, 20, 50, 100 and 500 euros; coins in 1 and 2 euros and 1, 2, 5, 10, 20 and 50 cents.

For currency restrictions, see CUSTOMS AND ENTRY REQUIREMENTS.

Banks and currency exchange. Most banks are open 8.30am–1.30pm and 2.30pm–4pm, Monday–Friday. In the south, opening hours tend to be later in the afternoon. Money can be changed at currency-exchange offices *(ufficio di cambio)* in main railway stations and airports and at privately owned offices, located around town. However, the exchange rate or the addition of a commission tends to make the latter's transactions less advantageous than those offered by banks. The same applies to foreign currency or travellers' cheques changed in hotels, shops or restaurants.

ATMS. Cashpoints *(banc-o-mat)* outside banks are widely available in Italy, and are much the easiest way of obtaining cash advances in euros, drawn on either your bank or on your credit card; they also provide a much better exchange rate than cash or travellers' cheques. Check with your bank at home to make sure that your account and PIN

I want to change some pounds/dollars/ travellers cheques.	**Voglio cambiare delle sterline/ dei dollari/ traveller cheque.**
Can I pay with this credit card?	**Posso pagare con la carta di credito?**
Where is the bank?	**Dov' è la banca?**
Where is an ATM?	**Dov' è il bancomat?**

number are authorised for international withdrawals. Look for correlating symbols on the cash machine and the back of your card.

Credit cards, travellers cheques. Most hotels, many shops, service stations and restaurants honour major international credit cards. Travellers cheques (such as Thomas Cook and American Express) are accepted in cities and tourist resorts. In small towns, (especially in the south) it's best to always have some cash handy. Take your passport or national identity card along whenever you go to a bureau de change *(Cambio)*.

O

OPENING TIMES *(orari di apertura)*

Banks are generally open 8am–1.30pm and 2.30pm–4pm Monday–Friday. Exchange offices at airports and major railway stations are open until late in the evening and on Saturday and Sunday.

Churches generally close for sightseeing at lunchtime, approximately noon–3pm or even later. They discourage tourist visits during Sunday morning services.

Museums and art galleries may change their hours from one season to the next. They are usually open from 9 or 9.30am–4pm, and in some cases 5–8pm Tuesday–Saturday and until 1pm on Sunday. Closing day is generally Monday. If Monday is a holiday, some museums and galleries close the following day. Check times locally before you set out.

Post offices normally open from 8.15 or 8.30am–1.30 or 2pm Monday–Friday, until noon on Saturday and on the last day of the month. Main post offices in larger cities keep longer hours.

Shops open 9am–12.30 or 1pm and from 3.30 or 4pm–7.30 or 8pm. In Milan, Turin, and tourist-visited cities, the lunch break is normally shorter and closing time earlier. Most shops close on Monday morning or Saturday afternoon and on Sunday. Food stores generally open earlier, closing on Wednesday or Thursday afternoons. Shops in tourist resorts or cities often stay open all day, every day, in high season. There are a very limited number of stores open during the month of August: if you see a sign that says *chiuso per ferie* with dates, it indicates that they are closed for holidays and shows the date when they will re-open. Many of the commercial shops in the centre have *orario continuato*, which means that they do not close for a lunch break and have a tendency not to close for summer holidays. Great shopping times in Italy are the two legal sale periods: from the second week of January to the second week of February, and mid-August to mid-September. Outside these periods, stores are not permitted to sell goods below the marked prices, according to government-set fiscal laws. When you see signs saying *saldi*, you have come at the right time.

P

POLICE

The municipal police *(vigili urbani)* wear navy blue or white uniforms with shiny buttons and white helmets. They direct traffic and handle routine tasks. Some municipal police act as interpreters. Look for the special badge on their uniforms. The *Carabinieri*, a paramilitary force, wear light brown or blue uniforms with peaked caps, and deal with violent or serious crimes and demonstrations. Their headquarters, the Questura, deals with visas and other complaints, and is a point of reference if you need help from the authorities. The *Polizia Stradale* patrol the highways, issue speeding tickets and assist with breakdowns (see also DRIVING).

Italy's borders, ports, airports and railway stations come under the jurisdiction of the national police *(Polizia di Stato)*. In an emergency, dial 112 or 113 for police assistance.

Where's the nearest police station?	**Dov' è il commissariato di polizia più vicino?**

POST OFFICES *(posta or ufficio postale)*

Post offices, identified by the 'PT' sign, handle telegrams, mail and money transfers. They are generally open from 8.15 or 8.30am–2 or 2.30pm (main post offices until around 8pm) Monday–Friday. They close at 11.45am on Saturday. Hours may vary.

Postage stamps *(francobolli)* can also be purchased at tobacco shops and at some hotels. Mail is notoriously sluggish; ask for Posta Prioritaria, an express service that costs just a bit more but gets to its destination much faster.

Postboxes are painted red; the slot marked 'Per la Città' is for local mail, 'Altre Destinazioni' is for all other destinations. The blue box is for international post.

Telegrams *(telegramma)*. All post offices accept domestic and international telegrams. You can dictate one over the phone (tel: 186).

Where's the nearest post office?	**Dov' è l' ufficio postale più vicino?**
A stamp for this letter/ postcard, please.	**Un francobollo per questa lettera/cartolina' per favore.**

PUBLIC TRANSPORT *(trasporto publico)*

Taxis *(tassì or taxi)* can be picked up at a taxi rank or ordered by telephone. Extra charges for luggage and for trips at night, on holidays and to airports are posted inside every cab. It is normal practice to round up the fare.

In addition to **bus** *(autobus)* services, some big cities operate trams/streetcars *(tram* in Italian). Naples has four funicular *(funicolare)* routes. Rome, Milan and Naples have underground/subway *(metropolitana,* abbreviated *metrò)* systems. Be aware of the infamous Italian *sciopero*, transport strikes *(see page 237)*. Where required, remember to punch tickets to validate them before boarding, or you will risk a stiff fine regardless of being a non-Italian speaker.

Buy **tickets** for buses and trams in advance at tobacco shops, newsstands or bars. There are Metrò ticket machines at metro stations.

Rome's buses can be crowded, but they are an inexpensive means of transport and a rambling introduction to the city. Tickets can be purchased in books of 10; one-day, three-day, and weekly tickets are sold at the ATAC (Rome's transport authority) booth in Piazza dei Cinquecento, in front of the Stazione Termini, the central railway station. If you are in a hurry, your tickets are also valid on Rome's subway (*metrò*). Lines A and B (with more than 30 stops) whisk you to a good number of Rome's popular sites. Remember to punch your ticket in both cases. **Horse-drawn carriages** have been a familiar sight in the capital – and other cities – for centuries. Fares are not fixed, so agree on a price with the driver before setting off.

Florence has about 40 main city and suburban bus routes. For information and a free bus map, go to the ATAF office right outside the central train station. Board buses at the rear and punch your ticket in the orange or yellow machine.

Milan is served by ATM buses and trains and the Metropolitana Milanese. Information and tourist tickets are available at the ATM office on the mezzanine floor of the Duomo metrò station.

In **Naples**, buses can be crowded, but they are the only means of transport in some areas. The convenient metrò connects the Stazione Centrale in the east with the Stazione Mergellina in the west.

Venice's water buses (*vaporetti*, and the smaller and faster *motoscafi*) ply the Grand Canal and shuttle between islands. Tickets can be bought from bars, kiosks and at most stops. Apart from single tickets (buy one and get it punched when boarding or you'll have to pay a surcharge), there are passes valid for 24 hours. The ticketing system is quite complex, so do check that you buy the right ticket.

Venice has about six water-taxi (*motoscafi*) stations. Although theoretically the rates are fixed, they tend to vary according to distance; clarify the destination when purchasing the ticket. This also applies to trips by gondola.

By coach. Italy has a vast network of coaches (long-distance buses) called *pullman*. Each province has its own company. Information on destinations and timetables are posted at coach terminals, usually situated near the town's railway station, and can be obtained from local or regional tourist offices *(see page 250)* or sometimes from your hotel.

By train. Children under the age of four travel free (unless individual accommodation is required); aged 4–12 inclusive, pay 50 percent. Apart from providing one of Europe's lowest fares, the Italian State Railways offer several reduced rates – see GETTING TO ITALY, page 235. Tickets can be purchased and reservations made at travel agencies and railway stations in advance.

Italian trains are classified according to speed. Best and fastest are the Eurostar rolling stock (first and second class require supplementary fare and seat reservations), which have their own ticketing windows at all stations. Others are classified as Intercity (IC; some first and second class require supplementary fare and seat reservations to be made one day in advance) and Espresso (E; some first and second class require supplementary fare and seat reservations). The Diretto (D) is a fast train making a number of local stops, and there are two local trains, InterRegionale (IR; first and second

When's the next bus/ train/boat/plane for…?	**A che ore parte il prossimo autobus/treno/traghetto/ aereo per…?**
What's the fare to…?	**Quanto costa il biglietto per…?**
I want a ticket to…	**Vorrei un biglietto per…**
single (one-way)	**andata**
return (round-trip)	**andata e ritorno**
first/second class	**prima/seconda classe**
I'd like to make seat. reservations	**Vorrei prenotare un posto.**

class) and Regionale (REG; second class only); both are very slow. Remember to validate your ticket in the machine on the platform before travelling or you will face a stiff fine.

By boat. There are daily car-ferry connections between Reggio di Calabria and Sicily, Villa San Giovanni and Sicily, Naples and Sicily; between Civitavecchia and Sardinia, Livorno and Sardinia; and between Naples and the islands of Capri and Ischia. Regular boat services link Genoa, Sardinia, Naples and Sicily and connect the mainland with Italy's many smaller islands. Ferries and hydrofoils also operate between towns and sites on the northern lakes of Como, Garda and Maggiore. For information on timetables and fares, apply to a travel agency or the regional tourist office.

By plane. Alitalia, the national airline, and other domestic airlines have flights between Rome and/or Milan and some 30 Italian cities and less frequent service to a number of provincial airports. Detailed information is available at travel agencies.

R

RELIGION *(religione)*

Although Italy is predominantly Roman Catholic, all major religions have congregations in the large cities. Check local newspapers for details, or ask at your hotel or the local tourist office.

RESTAURANTS

In theory, an Italian *ristorante* is supposed to be larger and more elaborate than a *trattoria*, but they are both restaurants, as are the simpler *osteria* and *taverna*. A *rosticceria*, originally a shop specialising in grilled dishes, provides tables for guests to eat on the premises. A *trattoria-pizzeria* serves pizza in addition to other simple meals. If you want a quick sandwich, pastry, or just an espresso, soft drink, beer or apéritif, head for a *caffè* or bar. A *gelateria* specialises in rich, creamy Italian ice cream.

Ask if the service charge *(servizio)* has been added to restaurant bills. It is customary to leave an additional 5–10 percent tip for the waiter. In cafés and bars, it will cost more to sit at a table.

When eating out, you are required by law to obtain a *fattura fiscale*, an official receipt indicating the sales tax *(iva)*. In theory, you can be stopped by the police as you leave the restaurant and fined if you are unable to present the receipt.

Waiter! /Waitress!	**Cameriere!/Cameriera!**
May I have the menu please?	**Posso avere il menù?**
Do you have a set menu?	**Avete un menù a prezzo fisso?**
I'd like to pay.	**Vorrei pagare.**
I'd like a/an/some...	**Vorrei …**
beer	**una birra**
fruit	**della frutta**
ice cream	**un gelato**
(mineral) water	**dell' acqua (minerale)**

S

SPAS *(terme)*

Italy has some 340 spas and health resorts that use thermal waters for rest, recreation or treatment. For information contact: Federterme, Via Piemonte, 39, 00187 Rome, tel: 06 420122.

T

TELEPHONES *(telefono)*

Orange public telephones are found inside tobacco shops *(tabacchi)*, on the street or in SIP *(Societá Italiana per l'Esercizio Telefonico)* offices, where you can also make long-distance and international calls. They are usually open 7am–10pm. Most public phones accept

Give me coins/a telephone card, please.	**Per favore, mi dia monette/ una scheda telefonica**

only phone-cards (*schede telefoniche*), sold in tobacco shops in different euro denominations; insert following the instructions. There are also pre-paid international phone cards, which require dialling the corresponding toll-free number found on the back of the card. To make an international call, dial 00, followed by the country code (Australia +61, Ireland +353, New Zealand +64, South Africa +27, UK +44, US & Canada +1), then the area code (often minus the initial zero) and finally the number.

You must insert a coin or a card to access a dial tone even when making a toll-free call. Be aware of exorbitant hotel charges for direct calls and service charges for toll-free calls on their phone lines. To place a reverse charges call or to make an operator-assisted call, dial the following:

In Italy	1795
International	170 (English-speaking operators)
Directory assistance in Italy	12
International	176 (English speaking operators)
Ambulance	118
Fire Brigade	115
Breakdown (road)	116
Police (*Carabinieri*)	112
Police (*Polizia*)	113

TIME ZONES (*fuso orario*)

Italy follows Central European Time (GMT + 1). From the last Sunday in March to the last Sunday in October, clocks are put ahead by one hour. When it is midday in Rome it is 3am in Vancouver,

What time is it?	**Che ore sono?**

6am in New York, 11am in London, 1pm in Johannesbrg and 8pm in Sydney.

TIPPING (*mancia*)

A service charge of approximately 15 percent is added to hotel and restaurant bills. If hotel prices are quoted as all inclusive (*tutto compreso*), the service charge is included, but not necessarily the IVA (VAT/sales tax); ask if you're not sure. In addition to the restaurant bill's service charge, it is customary to give the waiter something extra. Bellboys, doormen, bartenders and service-station attendants all expect a tip of a euro or two, depending on the situation.

Thank you, this is for you.	**Grazie, questo è per Lei.**
Keep the change.	**Tenga il resto.**

TOILETS

Toilets may be labelled with a symbol of a man or a woman or the initials W.C. The wording may be in Italian, but beware, as you might be misled: **Uomini** is for men, **Donne** is for women. **Signori** (with a final i) is for men; **Signore** (with an e) is for women.

Where are the toilets?	**Dove sono i gabinetti?**

TOURIST INFORMATION OFFICES

The Italian National Tourist Office (ENIT, Ente Nazionale Italiano per il Turismo, Via Marghera 2/6, 00185 Roma, tel: (06) 49711, fax: (06) 4463 379/446 9907, <www.enit.it> is represented in Italy and abroad. The organisation publishes detailed brochures with up-to-date information on accommodation, means of transport, general tips and useful addresses for the whole country.

Australia and New Zealand Level 26, 44 Market Street NSW 2000 Sydney, tel: (61) 02-9262 1666, fax: (61) 02-9262 1677, e-mail: <enitour@ihug.com.au>.

Canada 17 Bloor Street East Suite 907, South Tower, M4W3R8 Toronto, Ontario, tel: 416-925 4882/925 3725, fax: 416-925 4799, <enit.canada@on.aibn.com>.

South Africa London House, 21 Loveday Street, P.O. Box 6507, Johannesburg 2000, tel: (11) 838-3247.

UK 1 Princes Street, London W1B 2AY, tel: (20) 7408 1254, fax: (20) 7399 3567, e-mail: <enitlond@globalnet@.uk, <www.enit.it>.

US Chicago: 500 North Michigan Avenue, Suite 401, Chicago, IL 60611, tel: (312) 644 0996, fax: (312) 644 3019, e-mail: <enitch@italiantourism.com>. New York: 630 Fifth Avenue, Suite 1565, New York City, NY 10111, tel: 212 245 4822, e-mail: <enitny@italiantourism.com>; <www.italiantourism.com>.

W

WEIGHTS AND MEASURES

Italy uses the metric system.

Y

YOUTH AND STUDENT HOSTELS

Italy's youth hostels *(ostelli della gioventù)* – of which there are more than 50 – are open to holders of membership cards issued by the International Youth Hostels Federation. Cards and information are available from national youth hostels associations and from the Associazione Italiana Alberghi per la Gioventù (AIG), the Italian Youth Hostels Association, Via Cavour 44, 00184 Rome, tel: (06) 487 1152, fax: (06) 48 0492. For further information, check out: <www.hostels-aig.org>, <www.travel.it/hostels>, and <www.ostellionline.org>.

INDEX